CANDLEMAKING & DECORATIONS
A Step by Step Guide

Valerie Janitch

Hamlyn
LONDON · NEW YORK · SYDNEY · TORONTO

Published by
The Hamlyn Publishing Group Ltd
London · New York · Sydney · Toronto
Astronaut House, Feltham, Middlesex, England

© Copyright The Hamlyn Publishing Group Limited 1973

ISBN 0 600 31781 1

Printed in England by Cox and Wyman Limited, Fakenham

Contents

Beginning Candle~Making

Just a few centuries ago this book would have had to begin with a recipe along the following lines . . .

Materials: Tallow (equal quantities of
                  bullock's and sheep's fat)
           Spun or twisted wick

Method: Melt the bullock's fat in a copper pan: skim off bits of meat and feed to the dog. Mix with sheep's tallow, then pour into a channel formed by a strip of bark, placing wick along the centre. Leave to harden. If liked, insert a length of thin wire with the wick, extending above to hang from a beam in the ceiling. When lit, the candle will appear to float in the air (beware of hot drips falling on hair and clothing).

And of course, the smell was terrible!

Nowadays, with the advent of paraffin wax, not only are candles a lot more pleasant to live with – but they are easy and great fun to make. Candle making is one of those crafts in which you don't have to suffer a great many disheartening failures before you are sufficiently experienced to produce a satisfactory result. Your very first candle may not be perfect – but if you follow the simple basic rules, it should be good enough to give *you* a thrill of pleasure . . . and an enthusiasm to make more.

There are several very good books which go into the mechanics of candle making in great depth, including commercially. If you decide you want to study the subject to this extent, you will discover some of the really unusual and elaborate ways in which candles can be made. But I am deliberately covering only the basic methods of candle making, because I don't want you to be blinded with science when all you want to do is enjoy a creative and satisfying pastime. So all the candles you see illustrated here are made in improvised moulds, at minimum expense, using ordinary domestic equipment – the kind of utensils which can be found in any kitchen. Nor are they highly professional looking. That is the charm of the home-made candle: it *looks* hand-crafted, and will inspire much more admiration and flattering comment for being so.

But supposing you're *not* keen to go to the trouble of making your own candles—though you would still like to enjoy really decorative candles which look wildly expensive, but aren't . . . well, you can do that too! I have also included a section on decorating ordinary household, and plain, inexpensive coloured candles—the sort you can buy in any store. You'll be surprised how simple it is to create really exciting, artistic and original candles by adding a little decoration or ornamentation—often using nothing more than a packet of children's wax crayons!

Now to begin. First the basic candle—then variations to develop different effects—then decorating finished candles, whether your own or the cheapest you can buy—and finally, setting them off to the best advantage. Whether you begin at the beginning, or just come in at the decorating stage, enjoy your work . . . and the results. I am sure you will.

Step by Step to a Basic Candle

There are various methods of candle making, old and new. The most satisfactory modern method is a moulded candle made of paraffin wax, and this is the type I have used for nearly all the home-made candles in this book. It is simple, clean and quick. The basic instructions are few–so are the materials and utensils needed–and once you have made your first candle, there are endless exciting variations and experiments you will want to try.

For your very first venture into candlemaking, I would recommend buying one of the excellent introductory kits which are sold by candlemaking suppliers, craft shops and some big stores. These contain everything you need to make your first candles–and will have full instructions for you to follow, using the specific form of materials as they are supplied in the kit. Some kits are very simple and basic–others are more elaborate: take your choice, but the simplest will serve the purpose very satisfactorily of teaching you to make a candle.

When you have used your kit, and understand the basic principles of candlemaking, you will be sufficiently experienced to buy the various ingredients separately in the quantities you require–and you will probably be tempted to invest in unusual moulds and special dyes. But to return to our basic candle, the materials you will need are:

1. Paraffin wax
2. Stearin
3. Wick

1. *Paraffin wax* forms the major part of the candle: it is creamy-white, and can be bought either in block form or as a flaky powder. Although one can buy blocks of approximately 1 lb., I prefer smaller 1 ounce blocks, as these make it very easy to calculate amounts accurately–and also melt well. Similarly, the powdered wax is easy to weigh, and melts quickly.

2. *Stearin* (or stearic acid) is necessary to make the candle harder, so that it will burn properly, preventing heavy dripping and making it burn more slowly. It also makes the candle opaque–and shrinks it slightly, making it easier to release from the mould. To every ten parts of paraffin wax add one part stearin.

3. *Wick* comes in various thicknesses, according to the diameter of the candle you are making.
The three usual thicknesses are for candles:

> Under 1 inch in diameter
> 1 inch to 2 inches in diameter
> 2 inches to 4 inches in diameter

There is also a metal-cored wick, which is only needed when the wick has to be self-supporting and inside glass containers. You will also need:

4. A mould
5. A double saucepan
6. A kitchen thermometer
7. Plasticine
8. Cocktail or lolly stick or meat skewer
9. Cooking oil (optional)
10. Newspaper and paper kitchen towels

4. *Moulds* can be purchased in all shapes and sizes, made in plastic, glass and rubber, including ones for ornate, heavily embossed candles. But for your first experiments you will find plenty of inspiration around the home. Here are just a few suitable improvised moulds:

> Cream, yogurt, cottage cheese, cole slaw or similar cartons
> Fancy shaped margarine cartons
> Milk cartons
> Tin cans (without a rim)
> Toilet roll tubes
> Card mailing tubes
> Kitchen paper or cooking foil tubes
> Pill containers
> Frozen fruit juice canisters
> Jelly (jello) dishes
> Patty tins
> Foil baking cases
> Tea and coffee cups
> Pottery mugs
> Drinking glasses

. . . even egg-shells! In fact, anything with smooth sides will do, as long as it is strong enough to withstand the heat and weight of the liquid wax – and the shape allows the finished candle to come out easily . . . so the top of the candle must not be wider than the base! And for your first candle, choose a mould in which you can make a hole in the base for the wick (remembering that you will be making your candle upside-down, so the top of your candle will be·at the bottom of your mould). If you are using a tube which is open at both ends, close one end with a circle of card the same diameter as the tube, securely fixed in place with adhesive tape and sealed with Plasticine to prevent any leakage.

5. *Double saucepan* Paraffin wax should not be melted over direct heat. An ordinary double boiler or steamer is much the best, but a saucepan with a trivet in the base will do. Some people use a number of small saucepans, but I collect empty tin cans in varying sizes – soups, baked beans, tinned fruit, etcetera – and use these for melting the wax. Not only are they disposable when finished with, avoiding the tiresome job of cleaning off hardened wax, but one can also bend the can to form a lip for pouring – so this saves having to decant the melted wax into a jug. I'm all for economy in utensils to avoid mess and unnecessary cleaning up afterwards! I find I can stand three tins comfortably side-by-side in the top of my double boiler, allowing me to work with two or three colours at the same time.

6. *Kitchen thermometer* It is important to heat the wax to the right temperature to ensure a satisfactory result. Any cooking thermometer will do, as long as it is accurate.

7. *Plasticine* seals the bottom of your mould, to prevent wax running out through the hole round the wick: it also makes a steady base, so that the mould stands upright.

8. *A stick or skewer* at least an inch longer than the diameter of the open end of your mould is necessary to hold the wick in position in the centre of the candle (see diagram 1).

9. *Cooking oil* is very useful – though not essential – for greasing the inside of the mould to make the candle easier to release. I always use it, except in rubber moulds.

10. *Newspaper* should cover all your working surfaces. It is also useful for cleaning up purposes and wiping out the inside of pans and tins – though I use *paper kitchen towels* for this, and also for lifting hot tins of wax out of the saucepan.

Add a knife, fork, deep spoon or ladle, and scissors – and you're ready to begin.

MAKING A CANDLE
First prepare your mould. A small, four-ounce plastic cream, yogurt or cottage cheese carton makes an attractive candle, so I have used this as an example.

Make a small hole right in the centre of the base of the carton, and smear a light film of oil over the inside (this isn't essential, but I strongly recommend doing it). Thread a length of wick of the appropriate thickness through the hole, leaving about an inch free on the outside: then cover the base with a layer of Plasticine, to hold the wick securely, seal the hole, and form a steady base (see diagram 1).

Stand the carton upright and place a thin stick or metal meat skewer across the top of the container, resting on the rim. Tie the other end of the wick to this, making sure it is held straight

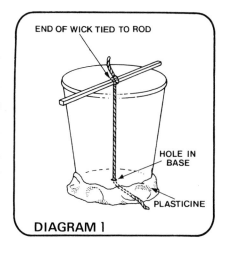

END OF WICK TIED TO ROD

HOLE IN BASE

PLASTICINE

DIAGRAM 1

9

up the centre of the carton.

Now melt your wax (you can be doing this while you prepare your mould, as long as you don't forget to keep an eye on it!). Put plenty of water in the base of your pan and then, over a medium heat, melt an appropriate amount of paraffin wax and stearin together in the top–preferably in a clean tin can (about nine or ten ounces of paraffin wax with one ounce of stearin should be adequate for a mould of this size). Using your thermometer, watch the wax until it reaches the correct heat. This should be:

a) For plastic and thin-sided cartons: not over 77°C (170°F)
b) For heavier-sided moulds: 82°C (180°F)
c) Never exceed 93°C (200°F)

If you want a coloured candle, add the dye to your melted wax at this stage (see the following section on adding colour).

Now either transfer the wax into a jug, or pour it directly into the carton (checking that the wick remains central). It is advisable to pour a small amount of wax into the base of the mould and leave it for a short while (checking there is no leakage), before continuing to fill the entire mould to just below the rim. Tap the sides of the mould gently to free any trapped air or tiny bubbles.

Leave the candle to cool and harden. The wax will take from two to three hours upwards to set, depending on the size and thickness of the mould. The process can be hastened by placing the mould in a refrigerator or under a cold tap or in a water bath, but this may cause tiny cracks and imperfections in the surface of your finished candle.

As the wax cools, you will notice that the shrinkage causes an air bubble to form below the surface. To correct this, pierce the skin three or four times round the wick with a cocktail stick or knitting needle, and fill the hollow with a little more melted wax. If you are making a large candle, you may need to repeat this topping-up operation several times.

Be careful not to unmould your candle too soon. When you are quite sure it is set hard, remove the Plasticine to free the wick, then tap the base of the mould gently to release the candle inside. If necessary, straighten the bottom of the candle by shaving away the excess wax with a knife to make it stand straight and steadily. Trim the wick and wax it ready for lighting.

ADDING COLOUR

Once you can make a candle, you will be impatient to use colour, since this is quite the most important factor in creating beautiful candles and artistic effects.

Colour comes in two forms–powdered, or solid "buds" of dye. Although the powder is more concentrated, I prefer the solid buds, as they are easier to use and control. The dyes come in the three primary colours – red, yellow and blue – and black: though you will undoubtedly find that your candle making supplier will offer a whole range of other shades too. However, it is possible to mix any colour by combinations of the four basic dyes.

Add the dye to your wax once it has melted (powder may be dissolved in a little stearin first, then added to the wax). Mix in a little at a time, shaving small quantities off the buds until you achieve your desired shade and depth of colour. Remember that red and blue make purple, blue and yellow make green, red and yellow make orange: add more or less of each colour depending which shade you want to predominate – and darken with black.

To test your colour, drop a little of the coloured wax into a small bowl of cold water. As it hardens, you can see whether it is correct, or what adjustments you need to make.

SOLID BASE MOULDS

Tea or coffee cups, pottery mugs, drinking glasses, bowls, jelly (jello) moulds, etcetera, all make excellent moulds to create interesting shapes. But of course, you cannot make a hole in the base to take the wick. To overcome this, you will need a *wick tube*: this forms a tunnel in the wax to carry the wick. When the candle is hard and has been released from the mould, the wick can be threaded through the tunnel in the centre.

To make a candle in this way, first plug one end of the tube (which must be longer than the depth of the mould) with Plasticine. Now cut a piece of cardboard slightly larger than the diameter of the mould: make a hole in the centre of the card just large enough to take the tube.

Prepare your mould and then pour about an inch of melted wax into the base. Place the plugged end of your tube right in the centre or the base, and slide the card over the top of the tube so that it sits on the rim of the mould, holding the tube upright and central. Allow half-an-hour for the wax to set, then remove the card, fill up the rest of the mould with wax, and replace the card once more.

When the wax is thoroughly set, remove the candle from the mould (lifting it with the tube), then remove the tube (hot water poured down inside the pipe will help to release it, if necessary). Thread the wick through the hole, then plug the base with Plasticine, stand the candle upright and fill the central hole with liquid wax, keeping the wick straight and central.

Alternatively, if you don't want to use a wick tube, you can make a completely solid candle, and then either drill a hole through the centre to take the wick – or make a hole with a heated steel knitting needle as the candle sets.

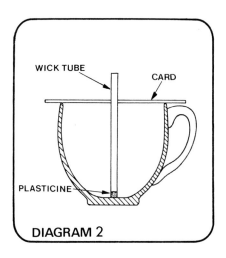

DIAGRAM 2

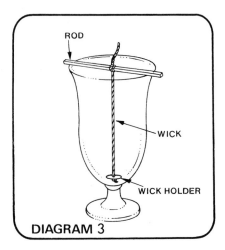

DIAGRAM 3

ROD

WICK

WICK HOLDER

GLASS CONTAINERS

Candles in wine glasses and other glass containers are not only extremely decorative, but practical too, if the candle is to burn in a draughty position. There are just one or two differences in the basic method to bear in mind–and you will need a *wick holder* and the *metal cored wick* mentioned earlier (this acts as a heat conductor, as well as holding the wick upright).

Thread the wick through the hole in the centre of the wick holder, then make a knot underneath and pinch the prongs of the holder together so that it is firmly gripped. Fit the holder in position in the base of the glass or container, then fix the top of the wick to the centre of a rod resting across the rim.

Stearin is not necessary for this type of candle, and the wax should not be heated above 82°C (180°F). When the wax is ready for pouring, remove the rod and wick and heat the glass in a bowl of hot water: dry it thoroughly, then replace the wick holder, etcetera, and fill the glass while it is still hot with melted wax to the required level. Top up round the wick as necessary. When hard, remove the rod and trim the wick.

Do Remember...
and Don't Forget...

SAFETY FIRST

First and foremost–TAKE CARE. Candle making is quite safe as long as you respect the fact that it *can* be dangerous–and are careful to observe sensible precautions:

Hot wax catches fire just like boiling fat. IF this happens, smother the flames with a saucepan lid or a sheet of foil: *don't* pour water over the burning wax.

Don't melt your wax over a direct flame–always use a double saucepan, and make sure the water in the bottom doesn't boil dry.

Never leave hot wax unattended–and keep it well out of the reach of children.

Don't let your wax get too hot: apart from spoiling your candles, overheated wax can give off poisonous fumes.

Take care not to splash water into your hot wax.

AND AFTERWARDS:

Cleaning up is much less of a chore if you are well organised and do it immediately you finish work:

Leave any wax that is left over to harden in tin cans or other containers for re-use–keeping different colours separate.

Wipe out empty containers and moulds with paper kitchen towels: this removes excess wax, and in the case of moulds which have been previously oiled, often avoids the necessity for any further washing.

Leave the water in your saucepan to cool, then skim off any wax before washing it–and all your other utensils–in hot water and detergent.

Any spots of wax on clothing or carpets should be left to harden, then scraped off before removing with cleaning fluid. *Don't* try to remove coloured wax from fabric with blotting paper and an iron–it may set the dye permanently in the fibres.

AND FINALLY
To end on a comforting note, remember that an unsuccessful candle isn't a disaster. Simply melt it down and try again–or if the experiment didn't work, use the wax for another type of candle. That's one of the great things about candle making: there's virtually no wastage of materials, even when you're still learning!

Special Effects

As you become more experienced, you will want to experiment in all kinds of ways to produce unusual and individual candles. You will probably have plenty of ideas of your own for exciting moulds and colour combinations: you may want to buy specially-made moulds from your craft shop—especially the rubber ones which produce those ornate, heavily embossed designs which are so expensive to buy ready-made. The more successful varieties you create, the more ambitious you will become: you can mould candles in rubber balls, balloons, egg-shells, crumpled foil, sand and clay, you can make them round crushed ice cubes or chunks of different coloured wax, you can twist and plait them, carve them and dip them . . . .

But even before you reach an advanced stage, there are many simple variations to your basic candle made in an improvised mould which will produce most effective results. Colour, of course, plays an important part, and clever combinations of different shades of wax can create beautiful and artistic candles. The simplest method is the one which also offers the most exciting possibilities—colouring in layers.

Layering

Make your basic candle in sections. Begin with the colour you want at the top, pouring in the wax to the depth required. Allow this to cool until the surface becomes rubbery: then carefully pour on your second layer of colour—and so on, finishing off the base by piercing and topping up in the usual way. The following candles can be seen in colour on page 19.

The squat blue and green candle was made in a mixed peel carton, filling half the mould with the first colour, then completing with the second when the surface of this layer was sufficiently set.

The taller yellow, orange and red candle was made in a half-pint cream carton, beginning with a layer of yellow, then gradually adding red dye to the wax before pouring each fresh layer, making it first orange, and finally deep red.

The big yellow and brown candle—made in a pottery coffee mug—was built up in the same way, beginning with yellow and then intensifying the colour until it became dark brown.

A small cream cheese carton made the yellow and green candle, gradually adding more blue to the yellow wax.

It is important to make each layer the same depth–or graduated depths–for this type of candle: so either use a scoop to measure the amount of wax you add for each layer–or mark the inside of the mould into equal sections to indicate the level to which you must pour each layer of wax.

Incidentally, if you tip your mould before beginning to pour in the wax–you'll get diagonal layers! You can either leave it in the same position throughout, or tip it at a different angle for each new layer (allow longer for the wax to harden for the latter method, though).

Whipping

This simple technique can be used to create some very pretty effects indeed. Heat your wax, then leave it to cool until it forms a skin. When it reaches this stage, whip it with a fork or a rotary beater until it becomes frothy like white of egg. When it is sufficiently whipped to resemble a fluffy meringue mixture, pour or spoon the wax into your mould, packing it down well and making sure the wick is still central.

You can see four examples of whipped candles illustrated in colour on page 19. The green one is made of green-dyed whipped wax packed loosely into the mould, then melted green wax poured over the top so that it seeps down.

The big pink and white layered candle is simply three layers of whipped wax packed down into a tall cream carton–first white, then pale pink and finally deep pink.

I used the remaining deep pink for the top half of the small cylindrical candle, made in a spice container: the lower half is solid wax of the same colour.

The brown and yellow mottled candle is yellow whipped wax into which I shaved brown dye just before it was ready to pour, only mixing it very lightly so that, although it was fairly evenly distributed through the yellow, it was only just beginning to dissolve. Then I packed the mixture down into the carton mould, finishing the base with a thin layer of melted wax.

Frosting

This gives a very attractive finish, which is particularly suitable at Christmas-time. It also serves to disguise a candle with a not-too-perfect shape or finish! The impressive candle in the picture (see page 19) was moulded in a mailing tube, then covered all over with frosted wax. White (or coloured) wax should be allowed to cool and form a skin, then whipped in exactly the same way as above. When it is fluffy as previously described, apply the whipped wax quickly to the surface of the

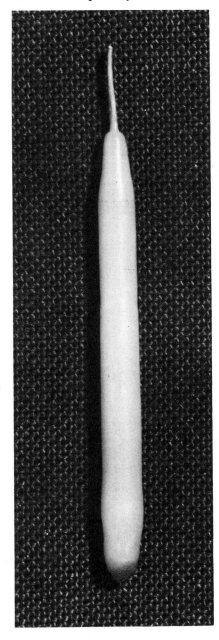

A dipped candle showing how the wax builds up in layers.

candle, using a broad-bladed knife or spatula. It is not necessary to add stearin to the paraffin wax when frosting candles.

Foil inlays

Pieces of crumpled kitchen foil or silver paper create a burnished inner sparkle, as shown in the brown candle moulded in a cream cheese carton (see page 19)–for which I used narrow strips of silver Christmas tree decoration. Place the foil or strips inside the mould, close to the sides and well away from the wick. Then fill the mould with melted wax, topping up and finishing off in the usual manner.

Scented candles

Perfume makes your candles even more pleasant to burn, and there are plenty of tempting possibilities from which to choose – ranging from the flowery rose, violet, gardenia, lavender, lilac, heliotrope and jasmin, through the fresh pine, cedar, eucalyptus and bayberry, the fruity strawberry, pineapple and lemon, to the exotic oriental sandlewood, amber and musk.

Try to colour your wax a suitable shade to accent the perfume – pink for a rose-scented candle, green for pine, yellow for lemon, and so on. Add your perfume to the melted wax just before it is ready to pour: you can also dip the wick in scent to intensify the aroma when burning. Remember that perfume tends to evaporate from the surface over a period of time, so it is a good idea to make the candle in a container of some kind. An apothecary, or similar, lidded glass jar is particularly suitable, and can be prettily decorated with ribbon and artificial flowers.

I made an appropriately scented deep violet candle in a wine glass (see page 19) – decorating the outside of the glass with a band of silver lace level with the top of the wax, to make it an attractive gift.

Incised patterns

You can make all kinds of interesting patterns on the outside of your candles simply by pressing a hot metal object against the surface so that the wax is slightly softened and takes an impression of the metal. I made a small plain gold candle in a little pill container, then achieved a rather rustic "corrugated" effect by pressing a steel knitting needle against it to form vertical lines all the way round, immersing the needle in boiling water between each application. (See page 19).

Dipped candles

The very first candles were made by repeatedly dipping a length of wick into melted wax, so that gradually the coats built up into a thick layer and formed a candle. This is fun to do, and makes a very home-crafted looking candle indeed, as the illustration shows.

16

Simply heat your wax in a can or other tall container to 82°C (180°F), then remove it. Tie a length of wick to a rod and dip it in the melted wax: take it out, pull it taut, then dip it again. Keep dipping the coated wick into the wax, allowing thirty seconds between each dip for the fresh layer to harden, until it is the thickness required. Leave the candle hanging until it is cool, then trim the wick neatly.

Incidentally, if you want to give a moulded candle a coat of colour or a smooth finish, dip it in dyed wax in just the same way, and allow it to cool before touching the surface.

A candle made from beeswax sheet. The top has been cut at an angle to give a spiral effect.

Beeswax candles

Long before paraffin wax was invented, beeswax was used for candles which were long and even-burning. Nowadays you can make a delightfully scented candle in minutes without even melting any wax, just using a sheet of honeycombed beeswax. These sheets come in a lovely natural honey shade, and an assortment of colours—I have used dark brown—and measure about $8\frac{1}{2}$ inches by 17 inches.

To make a candle like the one illustrated, first cut the honeycombed sheet of beeswax with a sharp knife as indicated by the broken line in diagram 4. Warm the sheet near a radiator or similar heater if it tends to crack, and press a length of wick along the longer of the two short edges, extending at each end, as shown. Beginning at this side, gently roll the sheet round the wick, keeping the lower, straight, edge level. Warm the shorter edge when you reach the other side, and press it against the candle to seal the join. Wax the wick at the top ready for lighting—and there it is!

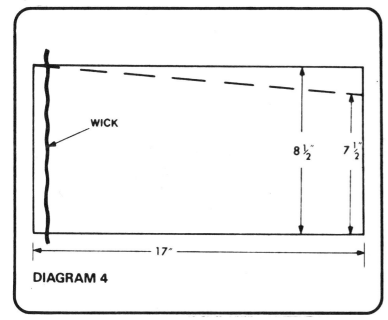

WICK

$8\frac{1}{2}''$ $7\frac{1}{2}''$

17"

DIAGRAM 4

Decorating Candles

The addition of just a little surface decoration changes a plain purchased candle from a rather dull, practical object into something eye-catching and artistic. It also seems to inflate the price beyond comprehension! In fact, some of the very beautiful candles one sees in the stores look too good merely to burn! So here are some suggestions for dressing up ordinary household candles–or the most inexpensive plain coloured ones–so that they *look* as expensive as those professional versions which leave such a hole in your purse!

The ideas fall into two categories. The first is a very simple method of melting children's wax crayons on to the outside of the candle–nevertheless creating some spectacular results. The second is just a stepping-off ground for a variety of surface treatments which you will want to develop in your own way to fit into the scheme and decorative theme of your own home. For that is the real beauty of candles: their light creates a focal point, softly picking out and emphasising the other lovely things which make your home.

USING WAX CRAYONS

For this simple technique you will need an inexpensive packet of children's wax crayons–it is important they are good quality, as the inferior kind tend to be gritty and give very disappointing results: and although you can buy smaller packets which are quite sufficient, a full range of about twenty-four colours gives scope for some really exciting and subtle colour effects. You will also need a small (old) pan of boiling water, a candle to work with, and a plain white one to experiment and develop your ideas on . . . and some kind of flame in which you can melt the surface of your decorated candle. I always use the automatic gas match on my cooker, but it can be a bunsen burner, a paraffin burner or even a cigarette lighter: or you *can* use your working candle, though this will give a slightly smoky finish which is, in fact, most attractive in some cases. Alternatively, you can substitute boiling water, but I don't find this method so satisfactory or easy to control.

The candles illustrated show all kinds of variations on this simple theme, but the method is always basically the same. Having decided on your colour scheme, cut away about half the paper surrounding the crayons you are going to use. Then,

(*Opposite*) A selection of candles, some plain, others showing examples of the various techniques used–layering, whipping, frosting, inlaying–and scented and incised candles.

A selection of candles decorated with wax crayons.

if using a dark colour, hold the tip of the crayon in the flame of your working candle just long enough to melt it sufficiently to dab on the candle you are decorating, so that it leaves a blob of wax on the surface. Continue to melt the crayon in the flame and dab it on the candle until the surface is covered with uneven spots of colour. If you are using a light colour, dip the crayon into a pan of gently boiling water: the candle flame will

usually make the light crayon sooty–though you may prefer this effect, in which case you won't need the pan of hot water. Repeat with the remaining crayons, dabbing on the new spots of colour between the first ones–until your candle is fairly closely covered with an untidy profusion of irregular spots.

Now, working over a sheet of newspaper to catch any drips, hold the candle in one hand and play the flame of your gas match, or alternative, on one section of the surface–just long enough to melt the spots and allow them to run into each other. Then quickly twist the candle and move to another spot. You will soon learn just how long to play the flame, and when to twist and move: if you find you have moved too soon, and the colours haven't merged sufficiently, you can always return. Continue gently moving and rotating the candle in the flame until you have covered the entire surface and are satisfied with the result. Leave to cool and thoroughly harden, then polish with a soft cloth.

Here are the details of how I applied and adapted this method to achieve the examples illustrated:

a) The tall, multi-coloured red, orange and yellow candle. This is made in exactly the way described above, using three crayons–dark red, mid orange and bright yellow–on an ordinary white household candle. I used my candle flame for the red crayon, but boiling water to melt the orange and yellow, to keep the colours clear.

I melted spots of dark green on a tall yellow candle to create a slightly translucent, under-sea effect. You will notice the colour grows darker and stronger towards the base, where I made larger and stronger deposits of green crayon. (Illustrated in colour on page 23).

b) The shorter yellow candle had vertical stripes of dark green, leaf green and lime green roughly melted on to the lower half, the lighter shades extending slightly higher than the darker. Then I ran the flame over the crayon only long enough to fuse the wax securely to the candle, taking care not to allow the colours to run into each other. Lay the crayon on quite thickly if you are decorating a candle like this.

c) The dark green candle with a fiery lower half also uses thickly encrusted crayon. This time I made a band of thick yellow crayon, added a narrower band of orange *over* the yel-low–leaving a strip of yellow above and below–and finished with a narrow band of dark red along the centre of the orange. Then I held the candle by the wick at the top and melted the lower half of the crayon–quickly turning it upside-down to melt the upper half of the band, allowing the melted wax to run right up the surface of the candle to the tip, so that there was no definite line where the crayon band ended.

d) The candy stick spiral effect makes a plain white household candle look almost good enough to eat! And it's as simple as it looks to make. You can, of course, run riot with your colour schemes: I chose violet, dark blue and carnation pink. I began by spiralling a line of melted violet crayon round the candle from top to bottom (leaving a space of about 2 inches between the diagonal lines). Centred between this line, I ran one of dark blue–then spirals of carnation between each violet and blue. I twisted the candle in the direction of the lines as I melted the crayon just enough for the adjacent stripes to meet.

e) The pale blue candle has its lower half heavily encrusted with silver. Use your candle flame to melt the crayon, and apply it very thickly, covering the surface of the candle completely. Then run the flame over the silver just long enough to fuse it to the candle, leaving the surface texture very uneven and irregular.

Of the two small, squat candles, the yellow one has short horizontal stripes of brown, overlaid with lines of black, melted and allowed to spread to form a rich, marbled finish. (Illustrated in colour on page 23).

f) And the deep purple one has a slightly impressionist-style flower design built up with thick encrustations of wax crayon in green, yellow and red–very lightly melted so that it adheres without the colours merging or losing their rough texture.

APPLIED DECORATION

Now for some inexpensive ideas for dressing up plain candles for an occasion. You'll find these–or similar–materials at your nearest haberdashery counter: ribbons, lace motifs, beads, pearls and sequins are available in such an exciting variety of colours and designs that the possibilities for unusual candle decorations are limitless.

The short, thick purple candle studded with pearls (see page 23) makes a rich and rare decoration–but is easily done. Simply heat the tip of a steel knitting needle, or similar metal point, in a flame, then press it against the surface of the candle so that it melts and forms a slight indentation. Quickly pick up a small seed pearl (I use the point of a pin to do this) and press it into the soft wax. Brush off any surplus wax and continue until the candle is studded all over.

A blue, forget-me-not-studded candle is created in just the same way. Any small artificial flower could be used–or suitable dried flowers. Cut the heads off the forget-me-nots (or alternative flowers), leaving about $\frac{1}{4}$ inch of stem. Then press the heated point into the candle–slightly deeper than for the

(*Opposite top*) A selection of decorated candles.
(*Opposite below*) A variety of attractive and decorative bases used to set off the candles.

pearls–and press the flower-head home.

A plain white household candle is quickly prettied up with a few attractive embroidered flower motifs. I gently heated the surface of the candle just enough to soften the wax so that I could press each motif in. For greater security I added a $\frac{1}{2}$ inch steel pin–but this is not strictly necessary if the candle is unlikely to be handled very much.

A chain of guipure lace daisies is another dainty alternative for a plain white candle. Just spiral them round, securing the first and last with a $\frac{1}{2}$ inch steel pin. Adjust the spiral so that it is evenly spaced all the way down, then anchor every second or third daisy with a pin in the centre.

Similarly, a length of embroidered ribbon spirals another candle–with a second spiral in the opposite direction to form a criss-crossed lattice effect. (See page 23).

And a spiral of silver tinsel braid looks dramatic on a plain black candle. Anchor with short pins as for the others. (See page 23).

The squat cerise candle demonstrates how easy it is to give a candle an elaborate sparkle with a few coloured sequins (see page 23). Beginning with a silver 'flower' sequin as the centre of the main motif, I surrounded it with ordinary silver-blue sequins to complete the motif: then dotted other sequins in assorted colours all over the rest of the candle. Fix each sequin firmly in position with a $\frac{1}{2}$ inch steel pin driven gently into the candle.

More sparkle–this time yellow beads picking up the colour of the glass in which the daisy-scattered brown candle sits (see page 23). A short pin through the centre of a bead holds each cream lace daisy in place on the upper half of the candle. Then a band of brown daisies circles the rim of the glass, stuck into position with fabric adhesive (or use double-sided tape).

And for a final sparkle–glitter. Although the usual way to apply glitter to most objects is to spread the surface with adhesive and then sprinkle the glitter over it, I find it more satisfactory to use heat when decorating candles with it. First sprinkle a little glitter on to the surface of the candle, then hold it in a gas match or similar flame long enough to melt the wax so that the glitter adheres. Having worked all the way round the candle in this way, go round again to give it a really thick coat. This prevents the glitter gradually falling away, as it tends to do if one uses adhesive on the surface of the candle. However, before setting the candle inside a plain glass in which it stands, spread the base of the glass with transparent adhesive and sprinkle more gold glitter inside, so that the bottom is glittered as well.

Setting Them Off

As long as there have been candles there have been candlesticks and stands, both plainly practical and elaborately ornate, in which to set them. And if you want to set off a pretty candle—or make a plain one look special—you can do a great deal by improvising an unusual base.

Plasticine is the steadying influence in all my examples, with—in most instances—a foil tartlet case forming the base. Although you can use ordinary foil—or for some of the designs, plain card—the tartlet cases are thicker than sheet foil, as well as being a convenient size and shape: and a packet of about fifty is not expensive. I begin by pushing a pin up through the centre of the foil case and into the base of the candle, then continue according to the finished effect I want to accomplish.

First a thick golden-yellow candle was fixed in a tartlet case as described above. Then I surrounded the base of the candle with a thick roll of Plasticine, moulding it down inside the case (diagram 5). This made a firm rim into which to press the gold-painted fir cones so that they were held firmly in position (see page 23). For even greater security, you can anchor them with a 1 inch steel pin—but this should not be necessary under normal circumstances.

The silver 'flower' sequinned white candle has a base made in the same way—but using a thinner roll of Plasticine. Then I twisted together some strands of silver foil Christmas tree decoration to form a 'cord', circled the base of the candle with it, and pressed it down into the Plasticine to hold it firmly (see page 23).

The red candle with a starched white ruff reverses the role of the tartlet case! (See page 23). This time I turned it upside-down, making a hole in the base through which I fitted the candle—round which I had previously wrapped an un-rolled paper chicken frill. A roll of Plasticine round the bottom of the candle, inside the tartlet case, fixes it firmly in position and makes a solid base (diagram 6).

Non-flammable Christmas floss makes a quick but very effective dark blue 'candle on a cloud'. This time I fixed the candle inside the tartlet case—then brought up the sides of the case all round, pressing them towards the candle and pinching

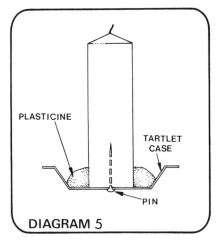

PLASTICINE

TARTLET CASE

PIN

DIAGRAM 5

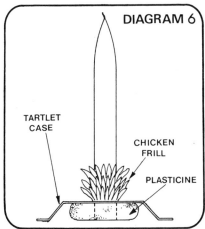

DIAGRAM 6

TARTLET CASE

CHICKEN FRILL

PLASTICINE

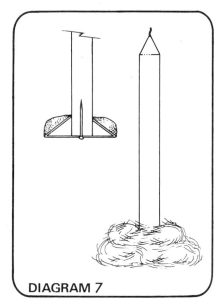

DIAGRAM 7

them together so that the rim was touching it–but keeping the bottom of the tartlet case flat. Over this I pressed a roll of Plasticine, to weight and steady it (diagram 7). Then I wrapped a length (6–9 inches) of floss lightly round the base as illustrated, completely masking the Plasticine and foil, and stuck the end with fabric adhesive.

I built up the base of a blue forget-me-not studded candle in just the same way as the candle on a cloud. But this time I pressed in short stems of the same artificial flowers which I had used to decorate the candle, to echo the theme by giving the impression of a bed of forget-me-nots.

Real or artificial leaves make one of the quickest and most effective base decorations to set off a plain candle. The sharp yellow candle (illustrated on page 23) contrasted by dark green leaves is good example. I made up the base exactly as for the previous two candles, then pressed in the leaf stalks–anchoring them securely with pins.

Any kind of attractive stone chippings make a good candle base. I used sea-green aquarium chips to put a dark green candle 'on the rocks'. As I wanted a fairly thick base of Plasticine to hold the stones firmly, I cut off the rim of the tartlet case, leaving just the flat base, before fixing the candle in the usual way and circling it with a thick roll of Plasticine. Then it was just a simple matter of pressing the stones firmly home, pushing them in as close together as possible, so that the minimum amount of Plasticine was visible.

Four yellow artificial daisies with brown velvet centres are all that is needed to make a white candle look as fresh as spring. I moulded the base on a rim-less tartlet case, as above, for this one, pressing and pinning the daisies neatly into place.

An olive-toned brown candle gets a sophisticated presentation with fir cones and dried grass heads. The base is the same as the previous two candles, the fir cones pressed in and pinned as before, and finally the short heads of grass stuck into the Plasticine between the cones. Note the matching gradation in the size of cone and height of the grass at each side of the candle.

Again I used just the same base for the stately purple candle encircled with matching statice flowers. Just break up the dried stems into tiny individual heads and then press them into the Plasticine until it is closely covered all round (see page 23).

Golden yellow and brown strawdaisies are a larger dried flower with which to create an artistic base. Follow the previous procedure, but stick 1 inch pins through the centre of each flower to ensure it is held securely.

(*Opposite*) Daisy Maypole–making instructions appear on page 38. (*Inset*) The Golden Harvest–instructions are on page 43.

A slice off a toilet roll tube can make a good base too! Cut off a piece 1 inch deep, then cut a circle of card the same diameter and stick it firmly over one end of your piece of roll with adhesive tape: to do this, stick a length of tape round the end of the roll, half of it overlapping the edge of the card. Snip this surplus tape into small tabs all the way round, then fit the card circle against the edge of the card and press the tabs down over it. Pin the candle through the base as before, then press strips of Plasticine inside the holder, between the candle and card, to steady the candle and weight the base. Finally, decorate the outside of the tube as required. I stuck a band of brightly coloured woven braid round one of my bases – adding another band to the plain white candle inside. And for the second example, I echoed the spiral of lacy silver gift-tie ribbon with which I had previously decorated a white candle, allowing it to overlap the top edge of the card base as illustrated.

For something completely different, a chunk of cork bark provides one of the most artistic and satisfying candle bases I know (illustrated on front cover). I embedded the base of my cheap white candle in a lump of Plasticine, then pressed it firmly down into position on the bark, making sure it was upright (steady the bark with another lump of Plasticine underneath, if necessary). Then I used four 1 inch steel pins to make sure it was held really securely. I finished my decoration with fir cones masking the Plasticine, but leaves, grasses, flowers and so on are all equally suitable for the purpose.

And of course one of the most attractive and popular improvised candle settings is a simple drinking glass. I encircled the base of a blue candle with statice heads stuck into Plasticine before fixing it firmly (using the Plasticine) inside a small brandy glass. Then I treated a similar candle in the same way, but lowered it into a tall glass of deep blue (see page 23).

I'm sure you won't want to copy my ideas exactly – but I hope I have given you plenty of scope to inspire a host of exciting developments of your own: the potential's all there.

Two decorated candle settings. (*Left*) stone chippings set in Plasticine and (*right*) pine cones and dried grasses.

Decorations for all Occasions

Before you even begin to look at this section of the book, I must emphasise one important point. To make them more interesting, I have related the majority of these decorations to specific festivals, anniversaries or family celebrations: but you will see for yourself how almost all the designs adapt easily for whatever purpose and event you have in mind. The basic directions remain the same – you will only have to make superficial alterations or adjustments to create your own very individual and personal decoration.

I have used generally available materials throughout – and if, in some cases, you can't obtain exactly the same thing, it shouldn't be difficult to find a suitable substitute. In fact, it is likely that your own ingenuity will improve on the original design! But do be sure to use the type of adhesive specified – it makes all the difference.

I have had such fun creating these decorations. Now I hope you will enjoy making them – and the final pride and pleasure of displaying the results.

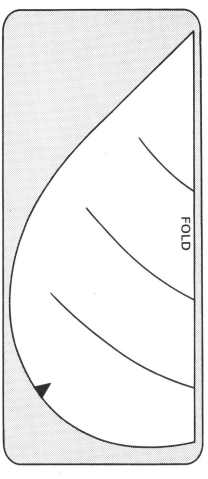

New leaves for New Year's Day.

(*Opposite*) The Bridal Procession
–making instructions are on
page 45.

New leaves for New Year's Day

Start the year right and turn over a new leaf with your break-
fast egg on January 1st! These disposable paper egg cosies take
little time to make – but they're an added incentive for all those
good resolutions: just be sure the resolutions aren't thrown out
with the leaves!

Materials: 3-ply green paper napkins
Matching cotton
Green felt pen

Method: Trace the leaf pattern from this page. Cut *four*
thicknesses of napkin for each side of the leaf.

Oversew the lower cut edge of each side between the notches.
Then oversew the two halves together all round the remaining
edges.

Mark a line down the centre, and veins as indicated, with a
dark green felt pen.

Saint Valentine's Ring

(Illustrated in colour on back cover)

A Valentine's Day greeting with a difference. Hang your heart
on the wall with this charming Valentine encircled in a
natural frame of dried grass heads. It's so pretty, your unusual
wall-hanging will probably stay there long after February
14th!

Materials: A 9 inch diameter lampshade ring
Dried grasses
A 5 inch square of deep pink velvet
Stiff card
$\frac{1}{2}$ yard 1 inch wide gathered lace
Artificial rosebuds and forget-me-nots (or
alternative)
$\frac{1}{4}$ yard narrow white ribbon
$\frac{1}{2}$ yard narrow ribbon to match grass
Fine wire
Tiny pins
Adhesive tape
Do-it-yourself adhesive

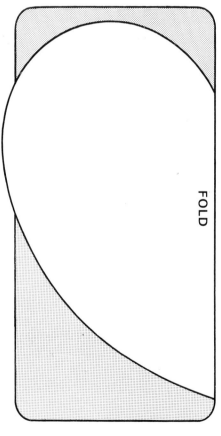

Method: Trace heart shape on folded paper: cut out and open
up to form pattern. Then cut in stiff card.

Stick the card to the back of the velvet, then trim the velvet
to leave about $\frac{3}{8}$ inch overlapping all the way round. Snip this
surplus into small tabs and stick down over back of card.

Stick the gathered top edge of the lace to the back of the card, so that it overlaps all round the edge as illustrated: gather slightly, or take in a tuck, at the bottom point.

Bind the flowers together to form an attractive group, then tie with narrow white ribbon and trim the ends. Fix to the heart with tiny pins hidden beneath the flowers.

Break off the grass heads and bind them to the lampshade ring with fine wire, adding each head separately, but making the frame two or three heads thick all the way round. Finish off neatly.

Fold the remaining ribbon in half and tie a knot 3 inches below the fold to form a loop. Divide the ends and tie them together round the ring, close under the loop, as illustrated. Then divide again and tape one end to each side at back of heart, so that it is positioned in the centre, as illustrated.

Twelfth Night circle

Twelve bright flames burn in a sparkling circle of silver and jewel colours. This original centrepiece is designed for Twelfth Night – but would make a tasteful party decoration at any time of the year.

Long-burning night-lights or – as in this case – the heating elements sold for food-warmers and hot-plates, supply the flames: the latter are particularly good since they come in packs of twelve, are cheaper than night-lights—and give out a really *warm* glow on a cold January evening! Or you could, of course, make your own candles—which would be cheaper still.

Materials: Stiff card
12 night-lights or alternative (see above)
A silver paper doily (about 9–10 inches in diameter)
Coloured foil papers (gold, silver, purple and blue—or alternative)
Plasticine
Clear all-purpose adhesive

Method: Choose a doily with a suitable design—if possible, the outer edge divided into twelve sections: place your candles on it in a circle to determine how they will look.

Cut a circle of stiff card slightly smaller than the doily, so that the edge overlaps the card all the way round. Cover the card with gold paper, then stick the doily on top: if the middle of the doily is plain, cut it away to reveal the gold underneath—perhaps finishing with a motif in the centre as illustrated.

Cut strips of foil paper $\frac{1}{2}$ inch longer than the circumference of the candles and fractionally deeper. Stick round the outsides, covering three in each colour.

Flatten a little Plasticine under the base of each candle to steady it, then stick to the base as shown.

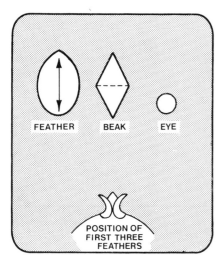

FEATHER BEAK EYE

POSITION OF
FIRST THREE
FEATHERS

A pair of little lovebirds

If you've baked a traditional Simnel cake for Mothering Sunday, this pair of nesting lovebirds makes a perfect finishing touch for the top. It's ideal for Easter too, of course–and appropriate for a Valentine cake–or an engagement party–a housewarming–or any other occasion when lovers get together!

Materials: 2 table tennis balls
Blue, green and yellow crêpe paper
Orange and black cartridge paper
Garden raffia
Wallpaper paste
Do-it-yourself adhesive

Method: Trace the feather shape from this page and use as a pattern to cut a large quantity in blue or green crêpe. Cut a smaller number in yellow. By folding the crêpe paper concertina-fashion (*along* the grain), you can easily cut six feathers at a time. The direction of the grain is indicated by the arrows on the pattern.

Using just a spot of adhesive at the base, stick three blue or green feathers close together facing each other in a tiny circle on a table tennis ball, so that they stand up in a little tuft (see diagram). Continue to stick feathers in close circles round the first three, sticking only the base of the feathers, so that the remainder is held up by the feather in front.

When you have completed about six circles, use a yellow feather in the next circle, to begin the underside of the body. Stick two feathers behind it in the next circle and so on, continuing to widen until the breast takes up nearly half a circle. Continue to stick feathers closely together to form the shape of the body, following the illustration. Then complete the yellow underside, narrowing quickly and ending to form the face, the base of the final yellow feathers covering the base of the last blue or green ones.

Trace the eyes and beak and cut in black and orange cartridge paper respectively. Fold the beak as indicated by the broken line, then stick the lower half to the face, with an eye at each side, as illustrated.

To make the nest, saturate strands of raffia with wallpaper paste and wind round to form the bottom of the nest, adding strips of raffia for the sides. You may find it a help to use the base of a small bowl to mould the shape. The diameter should measure about $2\frac{1}{2}$ inches. When finished, soak again with wallpaper paste, leaving a thick layer all over. Stand on a piece of foil in a warm place until thoroughly dry.

34

Spoons and flowers for Mother's Day

A charming way to 'say it with flowers' on Mother's Day – or any other day ... It shows how much you appreciate her cooking too!

I have made two versions, one with real, and the other with artificial flowers (dried statice – and daisies with deep blue forget-me-nots, respectively). Use whichever you prefer – the message is the same either way.

Materials: A small wooden spoon
Dried or artificial flowers
$\frac{1}{2}$ yard ribbon
Fine wire
Adhesive tape

Method: Arrange the flower heads to form a neat bunch to fit snugly into the bowl of the spoon: wire the stalks together securely, then trim the ends about $\frac{1}{2}$ inch below.

Fix to the handle, immediately against the bowl of the spoon, by binding with a thin strip of adhesive tape.

Tie the ribbon in a bow round the base of the flowers, to mask the tape. Trim ends of ribbon and spread flower heads out attractively, as illustrated.

Many happy returns gift tags

For birthdays, Mother's Day or any other time you are giving a feminine present, make your gift look really exclusive with a specially pretty tag. Here are a few ideas to set you thinking: they're little trouble to make – and well worth the effort.

Materials: Thin coloured card
Tiny artificial flowers ⎫
Lace edging ⎬ To trim
Paper doilies ⎭
$\frac{1}{4}$ yard narrow ribbon (each)
Adhesive tape
Do-it-yourself adhesive

Method: Cut a $2\frac{1}{2}$ inch diameter circle in coloured card.
    To trim with flowers, punch small holes fairly close together: thread a flower head through each, leaving about $\frac{1}{2}$ inch of stalk at the back. Fix down with adhesive tape.
    Stick lace round the edge, as shown, or cut pieces from the decorative edge of a paper doily.
    Punch a larger hole about $\frac{1}{4}$ inch from the edge and loop matching ribbon through it, as illustrated, for tie.

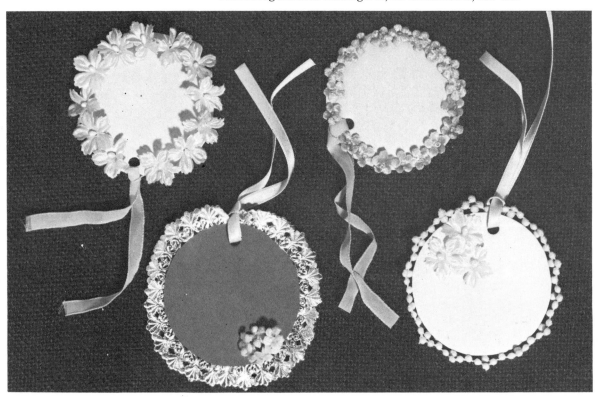

Chirpy chicks for Easter

A plain boiled egg suddenly becomes *very* exciting when it's a fluffy Easter chick! This is a quick and easy decoration to surprise and amuse the children. I robbed a feather duster for my bright yellow feathers–but you could cut them in crêpe or tissue paper as a substitute.

Materials: Yellow feathers (or alternative)
Stiff orange paper
Black paper (or self-adhesive circles)
Clear all-purpose adhesive

Method: Have the trimmings all ready to stick on to the egg when it is boiled.

Stick two or three short feathers together to form each fluffy wing as illustrated.

Trace the beak and cut in stiff orange paper. Fold it across the centre, as indicated by the broken line.

Cut black circles for the eyes, as diagram, or use self-adhesive tabs.

Stick a wing at each side of the egg as illustrated. Put a generous blob of adhesive on the centre of the fold at the back of the beak and press into position: then stick an eye at each side.

Chirpy Easter chicks and a selection of gaily decorated Easter eggs.

37

Dainty Easter eggs

(Illustrated on previous page)

There's nothing so traditional – or charming – as the custom of decorating eggs for Easter. Although you *can* just hard-boil the eggs, these ones are so pretty that the recipients are sure to want to keep them to treasure – so I've blown them instead.

Materials: Large eggs
Lace, narrow velvet ribbon, braid, pearls, beads, sequins, embroidered motifs, tissue paper, etcetera, to decorate
Wallpaper paste
Clear all-purpose adhesive

Method: To blow the egg, use a long darning needle. Scratch the surface at the pointed end gently until you are able to pierce a small hole. Then make a slightly larger hole at the rounded end. Push the needle inside to break the yolk, and stir it round to mix it with the white.

Hold the egg over a bowl and gently blow through the pointed end until the inside has all escaped. Wash the shell thoroughly in soapy water and leave to drain and dry.

Follow the illustration to trim the eggs, using the decoration you have available. To achieve the mottled coloured effect, paste tiny scraps of torn-up tissue paper all over the surface, the edges slightly overlapping. Allow to dry thoroughly before trimming.

Daisy Maypole

(Illustrated in colour on page 27)

Fresh as the joy of Springtime – pink and white daises dancing round the traditional maypole. This dainty decoration would draw appreciative comments at any time – but it's especially suitable for a Maytime birthday or other celebration, either decorating a sugar-frosted cake or, as I have shown it, as a centrepiece set on a silver cake board.

Materials: Plastic cake candle-holders
Pink, white and yellow crêpe paper
Green coloured paper
9 inch long thin garden stake (or knitting needle)
Silver foil
Cake candles
10 inch diameter cake board (optional)
Do-it-yourself adhesive

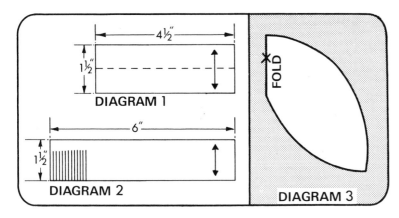

DIAGRAM 1

DIAGRAM 2

DIAGRAM 3

Method: Break off the outer petals or similar decoration round the candle-holders, and trim away the rough edges to leave just the basic candle-holder.

To make each daisy, cut a piece of yellow crêpe paper $1\frac{1}{2}$ inches by $4\frac{1}{2}$ inches, with the grain running as arrows in diagram 1. Fold in half lengthways, as indicated by the broken line, then snip this folded edge all the way along, making the cuts about $\frac{1}{8}$ inch deep and close together. Open out the strip carefully and fold over again *against* the previous fold: do not re-crease fold, but stick lower edges. Stick this strip round a candle-holder, so that the fringed edge slightly overlaps the top of the holder: keep the lower edge absolutely level.

Cut a strip $1\frac{1}{4}$ inches by 6 inches for the petals – in either pink or white crêpe – with the grain running as arrows in diagram 2. Cut straight down to within $\frac{1}{2}$ inch of the opposite edge, as indicated in the diagram, to form a fringe along the entire length of the strip. Then stick round candle holder, lower edge of petals level with lower edge of yellow centre. Stroke the petals gently between the thumb and blade of a blunt knife to curl them round as illustrated.

Trace a pattern from diagram 3 and cut the leaf shape in folded green paper. Open out and make a hole at X, then push the point of the candle-holder through and slide leaves up below flower.

Sharpen one end of the garden stake to a point, and then cover completely with foil. Cut three 12 inch long strips of pink crêpe $\frac{1}{4}$ inch wide and three strips in white. Stick the three pink strips together for 2 inches at one end, and join the three white strips in the same way. Then stick the pink and white side-by-side, slightly overlapping and stick this section spiralling round the top of the maypole, as shown. Cut and fringe a 1 inch deep strip of crêpe, and stick round top of pole, curling round as illustrated.

Assemble decoration on cake or board as shown, fixing the end of a streamer under each daisy, with a candle in each holder.

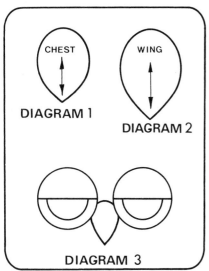

DIAGRAM 1

DIAGRAM 2

DIAGRAM 3

CHEST

WING

An owl for Father's Day

Decorating the cake for a male birthday or Father's Day is always a problem: but this wise old bird has all the answers. Basically, he's a hollow egg–so to be really practical, blow the egg first and use the contents in the cake!

Materials: A large egg
Brown, white and green crêpe paper
Brown tissue paper
White cartridge paper
2 pipe cleaners
Black and orange felt pens, ink or paints
Wallpaper paste
Do-it-yourself adhesive

Method: Blow the egg as instructed for the decorated Easter eggs (page 38)–or hard-boil it.

Tear brown tissue paper into pieces roughly $\frac{1}{2}$ inch square and paste all over the surface of the egg, edges overlapping. Repeat with a second layer of tissue: it doesn't matter if the finish is slightly wrinkled rather than completely smooth. Leave to dry thoroughly.

Trace patterns for the chest and wing feathers from this page (arrows indicate direction of grain). Cut nine chest feathers in white crêpe and stick the rounded top of each to the side of the egg (pointed end down), as illustrated. Begin with the lowest feather, then stick two side-by-side above it, three above those, then two again and the final one placed centrally much higher (leave this one until you add the face, if you prefer).

Cut seven feathers in brown crêpe for each wing. Stick these at each side, as for the chest, beginning with the lowest, then two above it, a central one above them, two above that and the final one in the middle again.

Trace the eyes and beak in one piece from diagram 3. Draw in black on white cartridge paper, colouring the eyelids and beak orange. Stick into position as illustrated, leaving the sides free.

To make his branch, cut $\frac{1}{4}$ inch wide strips of brown crêpe *across* the grain and bind each pipe cleaner tightly so that it is completely covered. Then bind the two cleaners together for 2 inches at each end, finishing off the crêpe strips securely. Divide the cleaners in the centre and bend these and the ends as illustrated, to hold the owl steadily in position.

Use the wing feather pattern to cut about nine leaves in green crêpe, and stick to the branch as shown.

Witches on broomsticks for Hallowe'en

Children always love a wicked witch–so for *them*, this is an any-time decoration. But if you're throwing a special Hallowe'en party, this dramatic mobile of witches with their black cats against a night sky will create just the right eerie atmosphere!

Materials: Papier maché, polystyrene or wooden balls, $\frac{3}{4}$ inch diameter
　　　　　Pipe cleaners
　　　　　Black crêpe paper
　　　　　Black cartridge paper
　　　　　Natural garden raffia
　　　　　Brown raffia
　　　　　Lolly sticks (about 4 inches long)
　　　　　Stiff card
　　　　　Yellow paper or poster paint
　　　　　Flesh-coloured poster paint
　　　　　Black cotton
　　　　　Twigs or a leafless branch
　　　　　Fabric adhesive

Method: To make each witch (I made five) cut a 5 inch length of pipe cleaner for the body, and $2\frac{1}{2}$ inches for the arms. Bend the body piece in half and push the bent end up into a ball. Tie the arm piece across the body just below the ball (diagram 1).

Remove the ball, paint it flesh colour and leave to dry. Cut a 5 inch diameter circle of black crêpe paper for the skirt. Fold in half, *along* the grain (see arrows, diagram 2), and cut a tiny notch at the centre. Push the lower half of the body through this central hole: bring the paper right up under the arms and push a leg inside each fold, so that the semi-circle of paper curves round behind the body as illustrated.

Cut a $2\frac{1}{2}$ inch diameter circle of crêpe for the cape: fold in half and cut a notch as for the skirt. Slip this piece over the top of the body and push the arms into the folds, bringing them together at the front so that the cape follows the line of the skirt.

Fix the head on top of the body. Cut a few 4 inch lengths of garden raffia and tie together at the centre: then stick the tied centre to the top of the head, bringing the raffia down over the sides and back.

Cut a 3 inch diameter semi-circle of black cartridge paper for the hat. Twist it round into a cone which fits the head *loosely*, then stick overlap. Cut a $1\frac{1}{4}$ inch diameter circle of paper for

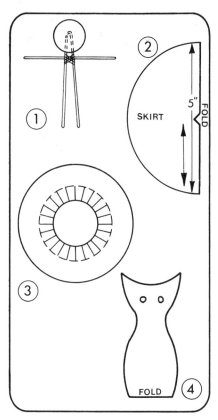

the brim. Measure the diameter of the base of your cone and mark a circle this size on the brim (broken line in diagram 3). Cut a small circle out of the centre, then snip tiny notches between this edge and the marked circle (see diagram). Bend these tabs up and stick inside lower edge of cone. Stick hat in position on the head.

For the broom, cut a bunch of 2 inch lengths of brown raffia. Tie one end tightly round the end of a lolly stick.

Tie an 18 inch length of black cotton round the broomstick, about 1 inch from the top. Thread a needle with the cotton and take it through the back of the witch's cape, close behind the head, and then through the back of the brim of her hat, close to the crown. Position her astride the broomstick and catch the back of her skirt under the top of the raffia (a tiny pin pushed through the skirt into the raffia will hold her securely in place).

Trace the cat and cut it *double* in folded paper, as indicated on pattern. Paint the eyes on one side only – or punch holes and stick yellow paper behind. Fold the base of the cat round two or three strands of the raffia on the broom as illustrated.

Cut a crescent moon in stiff card (using a radius of about 3 inches for the outer curve), then either paint it or cover both sides with yellow paper.

Tie twigs together to form a branch and fix in position as required. Then suspend the moon and witches from the twigs, as shown.

Golden harvest
(Illustrated in colour on page 27)

Capture the whole golden glory of autumn and seal your arrangement for all time inside a clear sparkling glass. Although primarily intended for a Golden Wedding, this exquisite decoration is a harvest festival in itself, and one which would grace any home all the year long.

Materials: A 1½ pint brandy balloon
An ear of barley or wheat, oats, straw-daisies, glixia flowers, grass heads, etcetera, all dried and either bleached or dyed shades of yellow, gold and brown
Plasticine
Transparent cooking film
Gold braid to trim
Silica gel crystals (available from chemists)
Pins
Clear all-purpose adhesive

Method: Roll a lump of Plasticine the size and shape of a golf ball, then flatten the base slightly. Pin a circle of straw-daisies all the way round, close together: push the head of the pin right down into the centre of the flower, so that it isn't visible.

Trim the ear of barley or wheat of its 'whiskers', then cut the stalk about an inch below the head, and push it into the centre of the top of the Plasticine mound. Now push a fine skewer or steel knitting needle right down into the Plasticine, close to the ear of barley or wheat. This is so that you can lift and turn the arrangement without disturbing it.

Lower the arrangement gently into the glass, to check that the straw-daisy heads are correctly positioned, and that the ear of barley or wheat is absolutely straight and not higher than the rim of the glass. Take out, make any necessary adjustments then re-check. Whilst it is in the glass study the position in relation to the shape of the bowl, noting the area where the greatest width is required – and how the arrangement needs to narrow. It helps if you, jot this down in a rough sketch (see the diagram).

Continue by beginning to build up the shape of the arrangement, adding the heavier heads and grasses evenly round the Plasticine, above the straw-daisies, so that they protrude at an angle to correspond with your sketch. Check once more inside the glass – and make further notes on your sketch to indicate how the rest of the arrangement should be shaped.

Cut short pieces of oats and the more delicate grass heads, and push them into the Plasticine, holding the stems with tweezers, so that they fill out the upper two-thirds of the

43

arrangement, as in the illustration.

Check these for height and width by holding the arrangement in *front* of the glass, to avoid damage by repeatedly taking it in and out through the narrow rim. You can see from the illustration that the most delicate grasses extend beyond the width of the bowl, so that they are held by the sides, curving gently upwards.

Finally, add the remaining heads and the glixia flowers to fill in the middle and lower half of the arrangement, cutting them to length and inserting with tweezers, as before. If the stalks are very fine, make a hole first with a needle or pin, then push the stalk down into it. Add a few more strands of grass, if necessary.

Wash the glass in soapy water, then dry and polish it thoroughly – especially inside. Tip a bare teaspoonful of the silica gel crystals into the base, then very gently lower the arrangement into the glass. Ease out the skewer or knitting needle, using it to persuade any awkwardly positioned pieces in the right direction.

Cut a circle of transparent film $\frac{1}{4}$ inch larger than the top of the glass: snip the excess all the way round, to form tiny tabs. Smear a little adhesive round the rim of the glass, then place the film over the top (making sure the under-side is free from dust or other particles), and stick the tabs round the outer rim, pulling the film very gently so that it fits smoothly over the top.

Stick the gold trimming round the rim over the tabs, slightly overlapping the edge, as illustrated.

Walnut boats in harbour

A very natural and unsophisticated table decoration for a family reunion. Thanksgiving for peace and plenty is symbolised in the tiny candle-lit boats safely home and bobbing at anchor in their sheltered haven.

Use an old shallow dish for the base, if you have one suitable – otherwise an earthenware plant-pot holder, as I have done. And make one boat to represent each person.

Materials: 5 inch diameter (approximately) earthenware
plant-pot holder or dish (as above)
Dried grasses, etcetera
Walnut shells
Birthday cake candles
Blue/green coloured stone chippings
Blue and brown Plasticine

Method: Build up the level inside the base with a thick layer of blue Plasticine.

Mould three mounds of brown Plasticine close to the sides and push a small bunch of grass heads into each, as shown.

Sprinkle chippings over the blue Plasticine so that it is entirely covered. Pour a little water over the stones.

Carefully split the walnut shells and take out the nut-meat. Fix a candle in the base of each half with a tiny lump of brown Plasticine.

Rest the walnut shells in position, as illustrated.

Bridal procession
(Illustrated in colour on page 31)

For a truly unique Wedding decoration, dress the bride and attendants with scraps left over from the actual wedding and bridesmaids' dresses: headdresses could be similar, too.

The basic figures are so simple to make that it comes as a surprise when you assemble the individual parts and realise just what a spectacular effect you have created!

I chose cream moiré for the bride, with cream lace trim and matching flowers (her lucky horseshoe is a cake decoration). Then I matched light and deep blue forget-me-nots to the

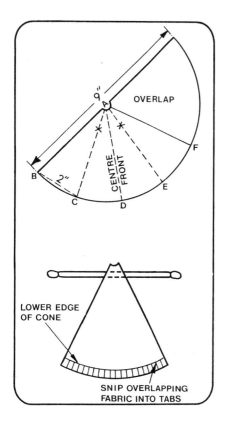

LOWER EDGE OF CONE

SNIP OVERLAPPING FABRIC INTO TABS

printed cotton of the bridesmaids' dresses. Any miniature artificial flowers would be suitable, of course – or you could use dried flower-heads.

Materials: 5 table tennis balls
Stiff paper or thin card
Fabric to cover
Narrow lace edging to trim dresses (15 inches for· the bride: 12 inches for each bridesmaid)
2 inch wide lace for train (1 yard – or less, as required)
Scraps of fine net or tulle
Artificial forget-me-nots (or alternative)
Double-knitting wool for hair
Silver horseshoe cake decoration (optional)
Pipe cleaners
Cocktail sticks
Pink corset lace or face tissue
Flesh-coloured poster paint
Black ink, paint or felt pen
Fine wire
Adhesive tape
Wallpaper paste
Clear all-purpose adhesive
Fabric adhesive (optional)

Method: To make the bride, draw a 9 inch diameter semi-circle on stiff paper or thin card, as diagram. Then draw a $\frac{1}{2}$ inch diameter semi-circle at the centre, as shown. With the point of your compasses at B, and a radius of 2 inches, mark the edge of the semi-circle (C). With the point at C and the same radius, mark D: continue for E and F. Place your ruler between points A and C, and mark X $\frac{3}{4}$ inch from A. Mark similar X $\frac{3}{4}$ inch from A along line A-E.

Cut out the semi-circle, cutting away the small centre section, and punch holes at X s.

Paste fabric over paper with the straight edge level with line A-F, so that the overlap is not covered. Trim edge of fabric level with edge of small inner circle, but leave $\frac{3}{8}$ inch overlap along A-B and round outer curved edge. Punch holes in fabric to correspond with paper.

Bend round to form a cone and stick the overlap behind, so that the straight edge A-F is level with A-B. Stick down the fabric overlapping A-B and snip the surplus round the lower edge into tiny tabs: stick these up inside base of cone.

Cut a $4\frac{1}{2}$ inch length of pipe cleaner for the arms. Push this inside the corset lace and cut the lace slightly longer at each end. Insert a little adhesive, press the cut end of the lace together and cut end to form a rounded, hand shape. Bind tightly with cotton $\frac{1}{2}$ inch above for wrists. If using face tissue, roll this round the pipe cleaner, stick straight edge and then finish hands and wrists in the same way. Cut a piece of fabric 4 inches by $1\frac{1}{2}$ inches for the sleeves. Roll this round the arms and stick the straight edge. Push arms through holes at top of cone.

Stick lace trimming round lower edge of dress, up centre front, round neck and wrists.

Pierce a small hole in a table tennis ball and push a cocktail stick inside. Paint with flesh poster colour. When dry, push the protruding end of the cocktail stick into the top of the cone, so that it drops *behind* the arms. Secure the end of the stick inside the cone with adhesive tape.

Wind double-knitting wool evenly round a 5-inch deep piece of card twenty times. Tie the loops at each edge tightly with a 6 inch length of wool. Slide gently off the card and tie the centre loosely with another piece of wool. Stick this tied centre to the top of the head, then bring the loops down, sticking at each side, and tie the hanging ends of wool tightly together at nape of neck.

Mark black dots for eyes, as illustrated.

Bind forget-me-nots heads together tightly with wire for bouquet, wiring in horseshoe, then bind to wrist and cut wire.

Wire flower heads together in the same way and stick to top of head, the stalks extending down back of head and hidden by the hair.

Cut a piece of net 9 inches by 4 inches for the veil: gather one long edge and draw up to measure $1\frac{1}{2}$ inches. Stitch or pin to top of head, round flowers.

For her train, gather one cut end of each of two lengths of wide lace and stitch or pin across back of shoulders.

To make the bridesmaids, follow the same directions, but draw your original semi-circle only 8 inches in diameter, so that they are a little shorter than the bride. Omit the front trimming on the dress, omit the horseshoe and use less flowers for her posy, but more for her headdress, spreading them out round her head as illustrated, and omitting the veil.

Arrange the bride and her attendants as shown, fixing the edge of the train over the bridesmaids' hands with tiny pins or stitches.

To complete the group, I rolled a thick white candle in silver ribbon, then pushed a wedding cake decoration into the side and filled it with sprays of lily-of-the-valley.

A detail of one of the bridesmaids.

47

Bride's prayer book marker

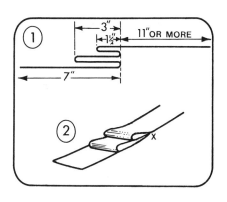

The bride wore white – and carried a simple prayer book, the marriage service exquisitely marked by trailing satin ribbons scattered with flowers and falling pearls . . . .

Not only does a decorated prayer book prevent a beautiful dress being hidden by an elaborate bouquet – but the bride can keep it afterwards as a treasured momento of her wedding day.

Materials: $\frac{3}{4}$ yard $1\frac{1}{2}$ inches wide double satin ribbon (at least)
3 sprays of white flowers (orange blossom, etcetera) plus leaves
3 seed pearls.

Method: Fold one end of the ribbon as indicated in diagram 1, then catch the two back folds (at broken line) securely together at each side, taking in the top layer of ribbon as well (X in diagram 2).

Lift the lower loop and make a small hole in the centre of the fold at the back. Push the stalk of a spray of flowers through the hole, so that the flowers emerge beneath the loop as illustrated. Catch the stem securely to the ribbon underneath just in front of the hole, and again just below the front of the loop above.

Lift the upper loop and repeat with another spray of flowers. Then make a hole in the top layer of ribbon, above the two folds, for the final spray: fix this in position, adding leaves to mask the top of the stalk.

Stitch a seed pearl to each loop, and one below, as shown.

Cut each end of the ribbon to form an inverted V shape, as illustrated.

Shower mobile

(Illustrated in colour on page 51)

The American custom of giving a bridal or baby shower – so that all her friends can shower the lucky bride or mother-to-be with gifts for the forthcoming event – is one of the most exciting things about getting engaged or having a baby. So what more appropriate party decoration than this feminine mobile!

Materials: A 12 inch diameter Tiffany lampshade frame
Lampshade binding tape
5 yards lace-edged $\frac{1}{2}$ inch wide ribbon
Narrow ribbon in 3 colours (pink, blue and mauve)
Forget-me-nots in 3 colours (as ribbons)
Small lace daisies (pink, white and blue)
Six 1 inch diameter silver lace daisies

(Opposite) Bride's prayer book marker.

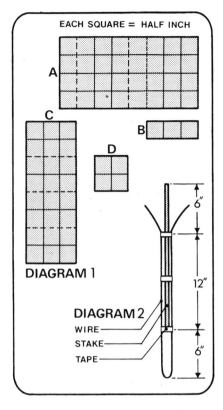

EACH SQUARE = HALF INCH

A

C

B

D

DIAGRAM 1

DIAGRAM 2

WIRE ———
STAKE ———
TAPE ———

6″
12″
6″

Silver tinsel cord (gift-tie)
Crêpe paper to match lace-edged ribbon
Gift-wrap paper (small, all-over design)
Wadding
Stiff card
$1\frac{1}{4}$ yards plastic-covered wire
18 inches long thin garden stake
Adhesive tape
Fabric adhesive

Method: First bind your lampshade frame tightly. Begin with the struts (it will probably have twelve – if not, adjust the decorations accordingly later on): then bind the top and bottom rings.

Make cardboard boxes for the 'gifts' as follows. Cut three pieces of stiff card 4 inches by 2 inches, and score as indicated by the broken lines on A, diagram 1. Cut three pieces of card 4 inches by $1\frac{1}{2}$ inches and score as C. Cut six pieces of card each as B ($\frac{1}{2}$ inch by $1\frac{1}{2}$ inches), and D (1 inch square). Bend each large piece of card round and join the short edges with adhesive tape. Then tape a small piece to fit at each side. Wrap neatly in pieces of gift-wrap paper 5 inches by 3 inches, then stick a length of ribbon round in each direction as illustrated, tucking a head of forget-me-nots under the join and tying it into position with one end of a 6 inch length of tinsel cord.

Stick lace-edged ribbon over each strut, then round the top ring. Stitch a silver lace daisy between every other pair of struts with black cotton, so that it hangs 2 inches below the frame. Tie each gift between the remaining pairs of struts, so that they hang 3 inches below the frame. Now stick remaining ribbon round bottom ring of frame.

To make the umbrella handle, bend $1\frac{1}{4}$ yards plastic-covered wire in half and fix it to an 18 inch garden stake as diagram 2, the bent end of the wire 6 inches below the stick, and the two ends free as shown. Beginning at the bend in the wire, bind with wadding to pad it as illustrated, finishing 12 inches up the stake, where the wire is free. Now cut a long, $\frac{1}{2}$ inch wide strip of crêpe paper *across* the grain, and bind the whole handle from the padded end to the uncovered stick, finishing off neatly. Curve the padded wire round to form a handle and trim with lace daisies. Fit the tip of the stick up through the lamp fitment and use the surplus wire to hold it in position round the small strut at each side.

Tie a loop of cord at the top to hang.

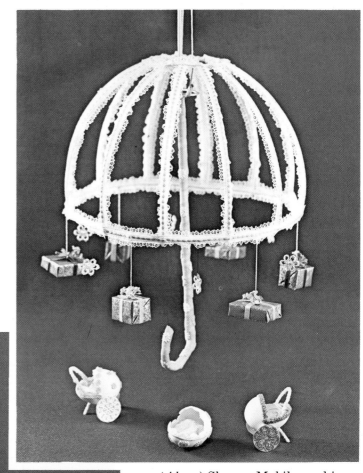

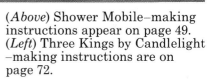

(*Above*) Shower Mobile–making
instructions appear on page 49.
(*Left*) Three Kings by Candlelight
–making instructions are on
page 72.

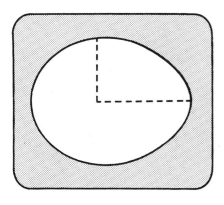

Cradles for the christening cake

The most charming decoration imaginable to mark baby's christening: tiny rocking cradles and oval baby carriages simply fashioned from delicate eggshells.

Materials: Large eggs
Lace or narrow braid, etcetera, to edge
Lace or similar motifs to trim
Paper doily motifs (optional)
Thin coloured card
Pipe cleaners
Cotton wool
Coloured face tissues
Adhesive tapes
Clear all-purpose adhesive

Method: To make the cradle, mark a pencil line halfway round the middle of the egg – a little nearer the round end: then mark a line at right-angles to the first one, round the pointed end of the egg (see diagram). Using a pin, gently scratch the shell along the lines until it breaks away: empty the white and yolk as soon as possible.

Wash the shell thoroughly and allow to dry. Then stick lace round the edge and decorate the outside with lace or similar motifs.

Push a little cotton wool inside, with a scrap of face tissue over the lower part to form the coverlet.

To make the baby carriages, follow the directions for the cradle. Then cut two $1\frac{1}{4}$ inch diameter circles in coloured card and decorate with circular motifs cut from paper doilies, for the wheels. Cut a 3 inch length of pipe cleaner and bend $\frac{1}{2}$ inch at right angles at each end, sticking this piece to the centre back of a wheel at each side. Stick the centre of the pipe cleaner to the underside of the cradle and bend each side down slightly to make the wheels lower.

Cut a $1\frac{1}{2}$ inch length of pipe cleaner and bend $\frac{1}{2}$ inch back: tape this to the underside, nearer the front, to balance, as illustrated.

Bend a 4 inch length of pipe cleaner round for the handle and tape the ends inside the shell as shown.

Finish the inside with cotton wool and a face tissue as before.

Coming of age

A really spectacular birthday 'card' to greet a young adult on the important day. You could, of course, successfully adapt this design to decorate the cake–in which case you would use cake candle holders with spikes: just make sure you use ten candles for the figure '1', and eighteen for the '8'!

Materials: A 12 inch or 14 inch square cake board
Dark brown paper to cover
Light green coloured paper (writing paper is excellent)
28 birthday cake candles
$1\frac{3}{4}$ yards narrow gold braid
A bunch of artificial daisies
$\frac{1}{2}$ yard $1\frac{1}{2}$ inches wide ribbon
Plasticine
Tiny pins
Wallpaper paste
Clear all-purpose adhesive

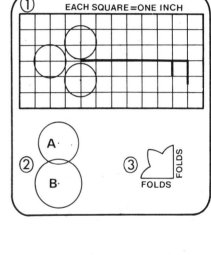

Method: Paste brown paper smoothly over the surface of the cake board.

When it is dry, mark the key and figures 18 following the diagrams to draw straight lines and circles: the squares equal one inch, to show where to place the point of your compasses in relation to the straight line for the key. With centre A, draw a $2\frac{1}{2}$ inch diameter circle for the upper half of the 8: then with centre B $2\frac{1}{2}$ inches below A, draw a 3 inch diameter circle for the

(*Opposite*) Top, Giant Tissue Chrysanthemums and (*below left*) the Wine-glass Cascade—instructions for these items appear on page 62. To the right of the picture is the Anniversary Rose—instructions are on this page.

lower half. The figure 1 is a straight line $5\frac{1}{4}$ inches long.

To make the candle stands, trace diagram 3 and cut in thin card to use as template. Cut a 1 inch square of green paper for each and fold it carefully twice—into quarters. Place the template on top, level with the folds at each side, and draw round it. Cut out and open up the paper, then punch a hole in the centre just large enough to take a candle. Fit the candle through, then mould a tiny ball of Plasticine firmly round the base and push the paper shape down on to it.

Stick two short lines of double gold braid at the end of the key, so that the cut ends are level with the long main line. Then cover this line, the cut ends at the top, between the two circles. Stick a single row of braid round each circle, then stick another row round the outer edge of the circles only.

Push tiny pins into the board at equal intervals along the lines marking the figures—ten pins for the 1 and eighteen for the 8. Then fix the candles on top so that the heads of the pins—protruding about $\frac{1}{8}$ inch—hold them securely.

Pin the bunch of daisies into position, then tie the ribbon into a bow and fix securely over the stems with pins.

Anniversary rose

(Illustrated opposite in colour)

A charming way to dress a table for any occasion, this delicate paper rose in full bloom is particularly appropriate for a wedding anniversary—especially if the celebration is just an intimate dinner for two.

If you haven't a collection of crêpe papers, you can, of course make a perfectly satisfactory flower using only a single colour for the petals and olive green for the leaves. But the shading *does* make the rose more effective, so do try to use at least two tones for the petals.

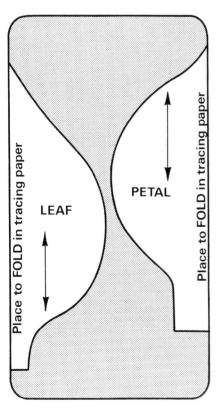

Materials: Crimson, rose and pale pink crêpe paper for petals
Olive and bright leaf green crêpe paper for leaves
Cotton wool
Solid adhesive in stick form (optional)
Do-it-yourself adhesive

Method: Trace the petal shape and cut in thin card to use as a pattern.

With the grain running up and down (see arrows), cut six petals in double crêpe—crimson on top, rose underneath (dull surfaces of paper together—shiny outside). In the same way, cut six more petals, this time rose on top and pale pink underneath. Finally, cut six more double petals in pale pink only—on top and underneath.

Anniversary rose and the patterns used for cutting out the leaves and petals.

(*Opposite*) The attractive arrangement of spiral candles, silver lace and kitchen foil for the Silver Wedding decoration.

Using solid stick dry adhesive (or a very fine film of other adhesive), stick each pair of petals together at tip, sides and base.

Now 'cup' the *lower* part of each petal as follows: holding the petal right side up, place your thumbs in the centre and gently stretch the crêpe so that it forms a cupped, petal shape. Then turn the petal over, and cup the upper half from the back, so that the tip of the petal curls over backwards .

Take a crimson petal and roll it lengthways quite tightly, inserting a tiny ball of cotton wool in the cupped centre and rolling the petal round it. Take another crimson petal and stick the base of this petal round the base of the first petal, so that they face each other. Follow with another crimson petal, the base of this only half-overlapping the base of the previous petal, lower edges always level. Continue as for this last petal with the remaining crimson petals, followed by the six rose petals, and then the six pink ones.

Trace the leaf shape and cut in thin card to use as a pattern. Cut five leaves in double crêpe – olive on top and bright green underneath. Stick together as petals and then cup as for petals – *but* begin with the lighter side up, so that the leaf is cupped and curled in the opposite direction.

Stick the leaves round the base of the rose and finish by binding neatly with a narrow strip of green crêpe.

Spread the leaves out as illustrated and open out the petals of the rose, re-cupping and curling if necessary.

56

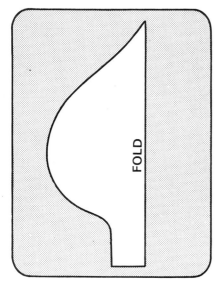

FOLD

Silver wedding

(Illustrated on previous page)

I bought silver spiral candles for this sparkling decoration to celebrate a Silver Wedding anniversary. But of course, this basic design lends itself to adaptation for any occasion: it could look very dramatic with all the candles in one strong colour – or better still, in different shades of the same colour.

The base is an old plate – it doesn't matter how cracked or chipped, since it is entirely covered by cooking foil.

Materials: An 8 inch silver spiral candle
Two 6 inch silver spiral candles
An old plate (about 7 inches diameter)
Silver cooking foil
1 yard 3 inches wide silver tinsel lace
Fine wire
Plasticine
Adhesive tape
Clear all-purpose adhesive

Method: Begin by covering the plate. Stand it on a sheet of foil (dull side uppermost), and cut the foil 2 inches larger all the way round. Bring this surplus up evenly all round the rim of the plate and then press neatly down towards the centre.

Gather one edge of the lace and draw up to fit about $1\frac{1}{2}$ inches inside edge of plate. Stick the ends, then distribute the gathers evenly and stick all the way round the rim of the plate.

Cut a circle of foil large enough to cover the centre of the plate and the edge of the previous foil, and the gathered lace. Stick into position, *dull side* uppermost.

Trace the leaf pattern on to thin card, and use as a pattern to cut nine leaves in folded foil. Open out, and stick three leaves round the base of each candle.

Make the crystal balls from foil too. Fold the corners of a $4\frac{1}{2}$ inch square of foil roughly towards the centre, shiny side outside: then roughly fold the corners in again – and crumple into a neat, round ball. Make a hole through one side of the ball with a pin, then thread one end of a piece of wire through, bending the tip back to hold the ball securely. Prepare three balls, on 3 inch long wires, for each of the two shorter candles, and four balls, on 5 inch wires, for the longer candle. Tape the wires to the base of each candle, between the leaves – fixing two balls together to form the back of the larger candle.

Roll a small ball of Plasticine for each candle: bury the base in it, then press the Plasticine firmly down on to the plate, positioning as illustrated. Arrange the leaves and balls attractively, as shown.

(Opposite) Flaming Candle Jars and Clowning Party Oranges capture the party spirit – making instructions for these items are on pages 68, 69.

58

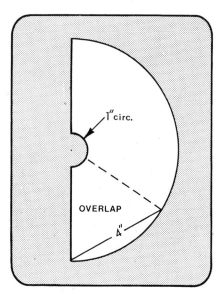

Golden angel for a golden wedding

Gold paper doilies and a table tennis ball make a quick table decoration for each place setting at a Golden Wedding celebration: silver doilies would make an equally pretty angel to carry the guests' names at a Silver Wedding. And for any party, dainty white doilies over a coloured foundation would look charming.

Materials: A table tennis ball
Gold paper doilies (about 9 inches in diameter)
Thin white card
Glass fibre decoration floss (or wool)
A cocktail stick
Adhesive tape
Flesh-coloured poster paint
Black ink, paint or felt pen
Tiny pins
Wallpaper paste
Clear all-purpose adhesive

Method: Piece a small hole in the table tennis ball. Push the cocktail stick inside, then paint the ball flesh colour and leave to dry.

Cut a semi-circle of thin card the same diameter as your doily, with a 1 inch diameter semi-circle cut away at the centre (see diagram). Paste doily to one side of card and cut level with the edge.

Curve the card round to form a cone, overlapping the straight edges about 4 inches at the base (see diagram). Stick join.

Fix the bottom of the cocktail stick inside the cone, sticking it to the back with tape.

Cut a 6 inch length of floss (or sufficient strands of wool) and stick across top of head, down sides and over back.

Cut a short length from the decorative border of a doily and fix across her head as illustrated, pinning into the ball at each side.

Cut a triangular section of doily and stick centre to back of body to form wings.

Cut a strip of white paper, stick decorative border across top and cut paper to follow shape of curve. Write name in centre and stick or pin to each side of body, as illustrated.

Draw black dots for eyes, as in the photograph .

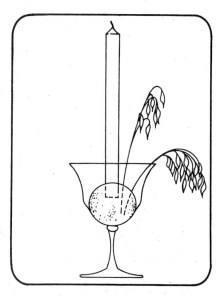

(*Opposite*) The Pirate's Treasure Chest—instructions for making this display appear on page 71.

Wineglass cascade
(Illustrated in colour on page 55)

I took a small plain white candle and melted dark and light green wax crayons together over the surface as described in the candle-decorating section of this book—to tone perfectly with the delicate falling greenery of this elegant table decoration.

Materials: A suitable wineglass (see illustration)
Dyed grasses, oats, etcetera
A small (5–6 inch) candle decorated to match (see above)
Toning Plasticine

Method: Roll a lump of Plasticine about the size and shape of a table tennis ball, then press it firmly into the base of the glass. Make a small indentation in the top and press the candle down into it, firming the Plasticine round the base so that it is held securely upright.

Break off short lengths of grass and stick into the Plasticine at an angle all the way round, so that they fall over the rim of the glass as illustrated. Then break off short lengths of oats (or more grass) and push into the Plasticine in a circle between the candle and the grass stalks, at a more upright angle as illustrated.

Giant tissue chrysanthemums
(Illustrated in colour on page 55)

Double chrysanthemums in glowing autumnal shades of brown and yellow make an impressive display in a simple vase on a coffee table or side-board. I used 'rainbow' shaded tissue paper, but plain tissue can still produce extravagent specimens—especially if you make the centres darker than the outer petals.

Materials: Tissue paper (as above)
Olive green crêpe paper
18 inch long thin garden stakes
Plastic-covered garden wire
Adhesive tape
Do-it-yourself adhesive

Method: Cut a 30 inch long strip of tissue paper 4 inches deep, and fold it in half lengthways. Then fold the strip in half in the opposite direction, then in half again—and again, so that it measures $3\frac{3}{4}$ inches by 2 inches. Hold the folded edges together and cut down from this edge to within $\frac{3}{4}$ inch of the lower edge, keeping the cuts fairly close together to form a fringe.

Unfold the strip and cut into four equal lengths. Then care-

fully open out the fringed fold on each piece, smoothing it flat and then gently bringing the lower edges together again, but *against* the fold, without re-creasing, to make a looped fringe: stick lower edges on each piece and then stick the four pieces together, one on top of another, along the lower edge.

Now loosely roll the strip up, sticking the lower edge as you go, and keeping it absolutely level (the centre will tend to ride up if you are not careful). This is the centre of the flower.

For the outer petals, cut another strip of tissue paper 30 inches long by 6 inches deep. Fold this in half lengthways and then fold the strip as before so that it measures $3\frac{3}{4}$ inches by 3 inches. Snip the folded edge to within $\frac{3}{4}$ inch of the lower edge as before, then open out the strip and cut in half only. Open out these two fringed pieces and stick the lower edges against the fold as before, then stick them together along the lower edge. Stick this strip loosely round the centre petals, using plenty of adhesive and pinching the base together.

Make a small hole with a pointed instrument through the base of the flower, from one side to the other about $\frac{1}{2}$ inch above the lower edge. Thread a 24 inch length of garden wire through this hole and bring the ends down equally at each side. Fit the tip of a garden stake against the base of the flower and tape the wire at each side to hold it in position.

Cut a long $\frac{1}{2}$ inch wide strip of crêpe paper with the grain running *across* it. Stick one end round the base of the flower, wrapping it round and round until it is completely covered, and then twist it round and down the stem, binding in the wires.

Trace the leaf pattern and cut two for each flower in green crêpe (again as arrows). Stick the base of each leaf round the stalk, one just above the other, and gently curl by stroking between your thumb and the blade of your scissors.

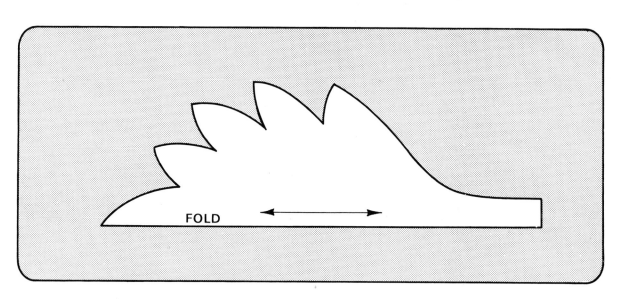

FOLD

'Bon Voyage' table decoration

When friends go off on a trip–whether it's just a brief holiday or a longer journey–it's a grand excuse for a party to wish them on their way. Here's an amusingly suitable table centre– radiating an appropriate method of indicating the seating arrangements!

Materials: Stiff card
Self-adhesive vinyl or coloured paper
A pipe cleaner
2 large sequins or studs
Small bunch of artificial flowers
$\frac{1}{4}$ yard ribbon
Coloured luggage labels
Coloured adhesive tape
Do-it-yourself adhesive

Method: To make the suitcase, cut a piece of stiff card 10 inches by 6 inches and score as indicated by the broken lines in diagram 1. Cut two more pieces, $3\frac{1}{2}$ inches by $1\frac{1}{2}$ inches, for the sides. Bend the main piece round and tape the two short edges together: then tape the smaller pieces at each side to form a box.

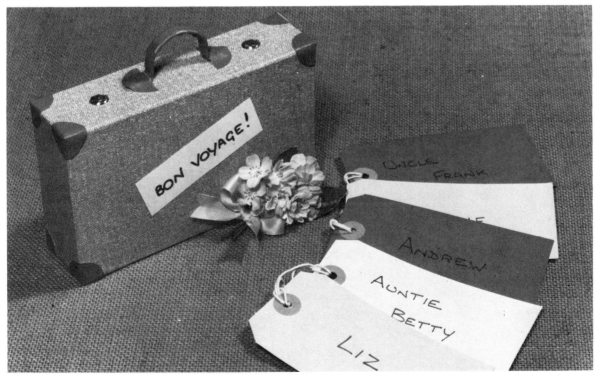

65

Cut a piece of vinyl or coloured paper 9 inches by $6\frac{1}{2}$ inches and stick to one side of the box, overlapping $1\frac{1}{2}$ inches all round: snip and trim the corners and stick neatly round to cover the sides. Cut another piece of vinyl or paper, $7\frac{1}{2}$ inches by 5 inches, and stick to the other side, overlapping $\frac{3}{4}$ inch all round: finish corners and sides as before.

For each corner, cut a 1 inch diameter circle of coloured tape and cut from the outer edge to the centre as the broken line in diagram 2. Stick to each corner of the box, overlapping the cut edges.

To make the handle, cut a $6\frac{1}{2}$ inch long pipe cleaner in half and lay the two pieces side-by-side along the centre of a piece of tape: bring one edge over and then the other, round the pipe cleaner. Then curve into shape as illustrated, bending $\frac{1}{2}$ inch at right angles outwards at each end. Cut a 1 inch diameter circle of tape in half and use to stick the ends of the handle to the top of the suitcase. Fix a sequin or stud at each side for locks.

Stick 'Bon Voyage!' labels on each side, and tie ribbon round the flowers to form a bouquet to place beside suitcase.

Write names of guests on luggage labels and place around the suitcase to indicate each guest's place at the table.

'Welcome Home' table centre

Here's an appropriate centrepiece for a housewarming or a Welcome Home party: the chimney gives away the inner secret of the tall residence–and proves there really is a warm welcome inside! Incidentally, this would make a novel wrapping for your contribution to a bottle party too: it's sure to delight your hosts–and make your offering into something really special!

Materials: Stiff white card
Coloured papers (red, brown, lilac, green and grey)
Sandwich marker flags
Tiny flowers (optional)
Do-it-yourself adhesive

Method: Cut a piece of stiff white card 17 inches by 11 inches and rule into sections following the diagram: accurate measuring is essential to ensure the house stands steadily. Score all the broken lines, cut the three straight divisions in the roof (unbroken lines), and cut away the shaded section at the top left corner.

Make two front doors as follows. Cut a piece of brown paper $3\frac{3}{4}$ inches deep by $1\frac{1}{2}$ inches wide and round off the top as a

$1\frac{1}{2}$ inch diameter semi-circle. Cut a $1\frac{1}{4}$ inch diameter semi-circle of lilac paper and stick to the brown as illustrated: mark into sections and outline with a felt pen, and draw a line across the brown just underneath. Cut the door in green paper $2\frac{1}{4}$ inches by $1\frac{1}{4}$ inches. Stick to the brown, then outline and mark into panels, etcetera, as illustrated. Cut a piece of grey paper $\frac{3}{4}$ inch by $1\frac{1}{2}$ inches and stick to remaining brown paper below door. Mark steps.

Cut fourteen pieces of brown paper 2 inches by $1\frac{1}{4}$ inches for the lower windows. Cut fourteen pieces of lilac paper $1\frac{1}{2}$ inches by 1 inch and stick to the brown pieces so that the brown paper overlaps equally at the sides and below. Outline and rule into $\frac{1}{2}$ inch squares as illustrated. Cut eight pieces of brown paper $1\frac{1}{2}$ inches by $1\frac{1}{4}$ inches for the upper windows and stick 1 inch squares of lilac to each, positioning as before: outline and rule into squares.

Stick a front door to two sections (so that they will be on opposite sides when the house is folded round), level with the

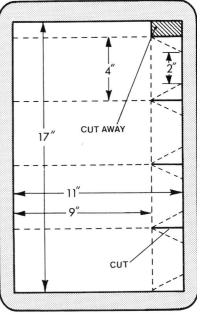

lower edge and $\frac{1}{2}$ inch from one side. Mark railings all the way round $1\frac{1}{4}$ inches deep and $\frac{1}{4}$ inch apart, using a felt pen.

Stick a large window beside each front door, as illustrated, with two more at the same level, equally spaced, on each blank side. Stick two more large windows on each side about $4\frac{1}{4}$ inches above the lower edge, with two smaller windows above.

Bend the walls carefully round and stick overlapping piece inside to join. Bend the triangular pieces at each side of the roof back and stick together inside to hold sloping roof in shape.

Cut two pieces of red paper 2 inches by 4 inches and stick to opposite sides of the roof: fold upper corners back and stick to roof sections between. Then cut two red pieces the same shape as the roof and stick over remaining sections.

Make holes in the card to fit flowers through on doorstep, and shortened sticks of sandwich markers at windows above, as illustrated – lettering an appropriate message as shown.

Flaming candle jars
(Illustrated in colour on page 59)

A quick, *very* easy and extremely cheap decoration to light a party – particularly an out-of-doors barbecue: the darker the night, the more effective will be the glowing jewel colours through which the flickering candles shine. Make them all to one colour scheme – or team various subtle colour shadings, as I have done.

Materials: Glass jars (1 lb size – about $4\frac{1}{2}$ inches high)
          Household candles
          Coloured tissue papers
          Plasticine
          Wallpaper paste

Method: Taking your tape measure across the centre of the bottom of your jar, measure the sides and base from rim to rim: for a standard 1 lb jam jar, this will be about 12 inches. Cut a circle of your palest tissue paper with a diameter fractionally more than this measurement.

Lay the circle on a flat surface and paste it thoroughly all over. Then place the jar in the centre and gently bring the paper up evenly on four sides: having done this, distribute the remaining tissue equally between, so that the outer edges of the circle are evenly gathered round the neck of the jar. Press the tissue smoothly against the sides of the jar with your fingertips.

Now cut a 6 inch square in your middle shade of tissue, paste it thoroughly, and then place the jar in the centre as before, bringing up first the four corners, and then smoothing the tissue between against the previously covered sides of the jar.

Finally, cut a 4 inch square in your darkest tissue and repeat the previous operation – positioning the corners of the smaller square between those of the larger one.

When dry, trim overlapping tissue round rim of jar neatly, and fix a candle inside with Plasticine.

Hanging barbecue light

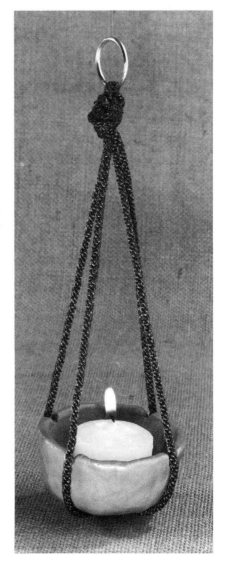

Primitive pottery makes a novel hanging candlelight decoration for a patio barbecue. Use self-hardening modelling material for the 'real thing' – or, if you prefer, model Plasticine round a foil baking case for a less permanent, but realistic, holder.

Materials: Self-hardening modelling material (or alternative – see above)
Deep yellow poster paint
$1\frac{1}{2}$ yards brown lacing cord
A curtain ring
A night-light
Clear all-purpose adhesive

Method: Take a lump of modelling material and roll into a ball: then make a dent in the centre and gradually push it down, moulding the sides round to form a small bowl, as illustrated. Try to keep the thickness as even as possible all round, and the top level. Rest your night-light inside, so that the top is just visible above the rim.

Make four notches in the rim at quarterly intervals, and a small indentation in the centre of the underside of the base. Leave in a warm place until thoroughly dry. Then paint with poster colour.

Cut the lacing cord in half, then knot the two lengths together at the centre. Stick this knot against the indentation in the base, then bring the four ends up on each side, so that each one corresponds with a notch in the rim. Stick lightly to the sides to hold in place.

Knot the four ends of the cord together and stitch to a curtain ring to hang. Stand the night-light inside.

Clowning party oranges
(Illustrated in colour on page 59)

Dress up oranges – or apples – in circus mood for a children's party. They'll be so intrigued by their zany clowns that your young guests will quite forget how good fresh fruit is for them!

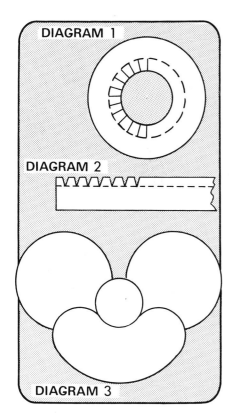

DIAGRAM 1

DIAGRAM 2

DIAGRAM 3

Materials: White and coloured cartridge paper
Patterned paper (gift-wrap)
Thin white card
Brightly coloured double-knitting wool
$\frac{1}{4}$ yard $1\frac{1}{2}$ inches wide ribbon (for each tie)
Narrow embroidered ribbon, braid, etcetera
Artificial flowers (optional)
Sticky stars and spots (optional)
Red and black ink, paint or felt pens
Tiny pins
Do-it-yourself adhesive

Method: To make the boater (hat), cut a 4 inch diameter circle of coloured cartridge paper, and mark a $2\frac{1}{2}$ inch diameter circle inside it: then cut out a $1\frac{3}{4}$ inch diameter circle in the centre. Snip all the way round the edge of this inner circle to the marked circle (diagram 1).

Cut a 9 inch long strip 1 inch wide for the sides, and score a line $\frac{1}{4}$ inch from one long edge; snip out tiny V-shapes to form tabs, as indicated in diagram 2.

Bend up the tabs round the inside circle of the brim and stick the straight edge of the side round them, joining the ends. Then bend the tabs at the top towards the centre.

Cut two more circles of coloured paper for the crown–one $2\frac{1}{2}$ inches in diameter and the other just fractionally smaller. Push the smaller circle up inside the hat and stick to the underside of the top tabs. Then stick the larger circle neatly over the outside.

Trim with ribbon or braid and flowers, etcetera, as illustrated.

Make the top hat in exactly the same way, but cut the circle for the brim $3\frac{1}{2}$ inches in diameter, with the two inside circles 2 inches and $1\frac{1}{4}$ inches in diameter, respectively. And cut the strip for the sides $2\frac{3}{4}$ inches deep. Decorate with sticky silver stars and coloured spots–or alternative trimming.

Cut a 6 inch diameter semi-circle for the pointed hat and curve round to form a cone with a 3 inch overlap at the lower edge: stick join. Trim with flowers or alternative as illustrated.

To make each tuft of hair, wind double-knitting wool loosely ten or twelve times round two fingers: tie the loops with matching wool. Stick under hat brims, or stitch at each side of pointed hat, as shown.

Cut a 1 inch wide strip of thin white card 8 inches long for each collar. Bend round to form a circle and stick a 1 inch overlap to join. Cut the ribbon into two pieces, one 8 inches long and the other 1 inch. Fold the longer piece so that the cut ends overlap at the centre back: gather straight across the ribbon, through the three thicknesses, then draw up tightly. Fold remaining ribbon widthways into three: wrap round the gathers and secure at the back. Stick bow to front of collar.

Trace the basic face from this page and draw a heavy black outline on thick white paper. Colour the nose red, then add eyes, eyelashes and mouth, altering the expressions as illustrated. Cut out carefully, then stick lightly to orange.

Sit each orange on a collar, and fix hats with a tiny pin at each side.

Pirate's treasure chest

(Illustrated in colour on page 63)

The pirate captain's hidden treasure reveals itself for a children's party – gold-wrapped chocolate coins tumble from a heavy antique chest. And you don't have to search further than your kitchen to find the secret – it's ordinary cooking foil.

Materials: Stiff card
Thin card
Silver cooking foil
Medium-weight piping cord
Black ink or paint (optional)
Adhesive tape
Do-it-yourself adhesive

Method: To make the box, cut two pieces of thick card 4 inches by 2 inches for the front and back, and two pieces $2\frac{1}{2}$ inches by 2 inches for the sides: also one piece, 4 inches by $2\frac{1}{2}$ inches for the base. Tape the sides together at each corner and then tape the base into position.

For the lid, cut a $2\frac{3}{4}$ inch diameter circle of thick card, then rule two lines $2\frac{1}{2}$ inches long, as diagram 1, and cut to form the curved section at each side. Cut the top of the lid in *thin* card, $4\frac{1}{2}$ inches by $3\frac{1}{4}$ inches: score $\frac{1}{4}$ inch from each side, as indicated by the broken lines in diagram 2, then snip the excess into tiny tabs, as shown.

Mark the centre on the card for the lid and then stick piping cord to form an abstract raised design all over the card, but not closer than $\frac{1}{2}$ inch from the edge. Now stick cord all round the edge.

Cut a piece of foil about 1 inch larger all round, then smear a little adhesive over the centre part of your design and press the foil over it, shiny side down, overlapping equally on all sides. Gently smooth the foil with your fingertips so that it wrinkles and takes the shape of the piping cord underneath: always push the foil towards the centre, so that it doesn't stretch and tear. When the centre is done, lift the foil at each corner, smear adhesive on the card, and then finish smoothing the foil over the main design and then the raised edge.

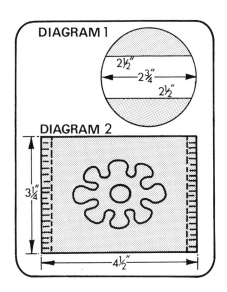

DIAGRAM 1

$2\frac{1}{2}''$

$2\frac{3}{4}''$

$2\frac{1}{2}''$

DIAGRAM 2

$3\frac{1}{4}''$

$4\frac{1}{2}''$

Bend the scored tabs down at each side and stick neatly round the curved edge of the two end pieces. Then bring the surplus foil down and stick smoothly over the ends. Stick the foil overlapping the front and back edges of the lid neatly up inside. Cut two pieces of foil the same shape as the ends, but about 1 inch deeper and stick at each side to neaten, sticking the excess up inside the lid.

For the front and back of the box, cut two pieces of thin card 4 inches by 2 inches. Make a design in piping cord on the main part and round the edge of each, as before: then cover with foil, overlapping 1 inch all round. Stick these pieces to the front and back of the box, sticking the overlapping foil at each side to the sides of the box, and at the top and bottom, inside the box and underneath, respectively.

For the sides, cut two pieces of thin card $2\frac{1}{2}$ inches by 2 inches. Make a design and cover with foil as before, but fold the excess foil at each side round and stick to the back of the card: then stick to the sides of the box, finishing the overlapping foil at top and bottom inside and underneath the box, as before.

Stick a piece of foil to the base of the box, then stick pieces inside to line the box and the lid.

Stick a piece of tape across the back of the box, half overlapping the top edge, sticking this half inside the back edge of the lid, to form a hinge.

To 'antique' the outside, soak a little black ink or paint into a small wad of cotton wool: then rub it all over the surface, working it well into the crevices so that it picks out the design in further relief. Continue rubbing to remove any excess ink or paint and the desired effect is achieved.

Fill the chest with chocolate coins or other bounty!

Three Kings by candlelight
(Illustrated in colour on page 51)

The magnificence of the Wise Men is highlighted by three tall, absolutely plain candles reflecting the colours of the figures. This simple-to-make decoration emphasises the power of wallpaper paste: it's the secret ingredient behind those elaborate costumes and draped headdresses!

Materials: 3 table tennis balls
Heavy cartridge paper
Fine printed silk or cotton fabrics
5 inch square of fine white cotton or paper napkin
Coloured foil paper (gold – silver – blue – purple)
Narrow tinsel braid (to match)
5 inches $\frac{3}{4}$ inch wide gilt braid
3-ply or 4-ply knitting wool for beards

72

Cotton wool
Diamanté 'jewels'
3 cocktail sticks
Flesh-coloured poster paint
Black ink, paint or felt pen
Plasticine
Adhesive tape
Wallpaper paste
Clear all-purpose adhesive

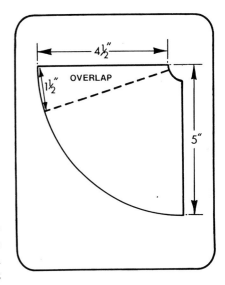

Method: For each figure cut a 5 inch radius quarter-circle, with a $\frac{1}{2}$ inch radius section cut away at the corner (diagram 1): mark a $1\frac{1}{2}$ inch overlap on the wrong side, as indicated.

Paste the other side of the paper to the wrong side of a piece of patterned fabric. When dry, trim the fabric level with one straight edge of the paper, and the inner curve, but leave $\frac{1}{4}$ inch of fabric overlapping the outer curved edge and the straight edge of the overlap. Curve round to form a cone and stick overlap, to join. Paste down surplus fabric along overlap edge, and cut the fabric round the base into tabs, then stick up inside the cone. Trim the lower edge with tinsel braid.

Make a small hole in a table tennis ball and push a cocktail stick inside for each head, then paint with poster colour. When dry, push the cocktail stick down inside the cone and fix to the back with adhesive tape.

Cut a quarter-circle of foil paper for each cloak, the same size and shape as the body cone, but making the inner circle only $\frac{1}{4}$ inch radius. Cut a narrow strip of tape $1\frac{1}{2}$ inches long and use to stick the cloak round the neck of the cone so that it hangs as illustrated. Mask the tape with tinsel braid.

To make the crown headdress, saturate white fabric or paper napkin with paste and drape over head as shown. Stick the cut ends of a 5 inch length of gilt braid to form a circle and stick over covered head, positioned as illustrated.

For the tall, steeple headdress, cut a 5 inch diameter semi-circle of foil paper and curve round into a cone to fit the head. Stick overlap and then stick to head at the angle shown. Cut a strip of fine fabric 6 inches by 2 inches. Saturate with wallpaper paste, then make a double twist at the centre (so that the right side of the fabric is uppermost at each side) and drape round head and lower edge of cone, as illustrated, joining the ends at the back. Stick diamanté jewel or similar trimming at the front.

Stick a small ball of cotton wool to the top of the head for the turban. Then saturate a 4 inch diameter circle of fine fabric in wallpaper paste, drape it over the top of the cotton wool and stick the edge of the fabric to the head all the way round. Cut a strip of the same fabric 6 inches by 2 inches and complete the lower part of the turban as described for the previous headdress.

A detail of one of the three kings.

Stick cotton wool to the lower part of the face for one beard, binding the centre of a tiny wisp of cotton wool tightly with white cotton for his moustache. Wrap plain or textured knitting wool loosely round two fingers about fifteen times for the other beards. Tie the loops with wool, then stick to faces as illustrated. Mark black spots for eyes, as shown.

Weight the figures so that they will stand steadily, with a strip of Plasticine round the lower edge inside the cone.

The fairy on the tree

Every little girl's dream fairy princess tops the tree all through Christmas – and flies down afterwards to grant her lucky admirer's wish.

Her dress is quickly made from triple-frill lace. You can either buy this ready made – or make your own: gather 1 inch wide lace and then stitch to a 2 inch deep piece of net, beginning with the top edge of the bottom row of lace along the lower edge of the net – then the two rows above positioned so that the bottom edge of each just overlaps the top edge of the frill below.

Materials: $\frac{3}{4}$ yard 3 inch deep triple-frilled lace
$\frac{1}{2}$ yard 1 inch wide flat lace
Six inches 3 inches wide tinsel lace (for wings)
$\frac{1}{4}$ yard $\frac{1}{2}$ inch wide silver lace edging
A table tennis ball
3 pipe cleaners
A cocktail stick
3-ply or 4-ply brown knitting wool
Pink face tissue
Flesh-coloured poster paint
Black ink, paint or felt pen
Tiny pins
Clear all-purpose adhesive

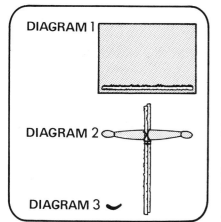

DIAGRAM 1

DIAGRAM 2

DIAGRAM 3

Method: To make the arms, cut a pink face tissue in half and stick a 5 inch length of pipe cleaner along the cut edge – then trim away tissue at each side to overlap the ends of the pipe cleaner $\frac{1}{4}$ inch (diagram 1). Roll the tissue round the pipe cleaner and stick joins. Then push a little adhesive up each end, squeeze together and cut off corners to form shape of hand. Tie tightly with cotton $\frac{1}{2}$ inch above, for wrist.

Tie two $6\frac{1}{2}$ inch pipe cleaners together 2 inches from one end, for the body. Insert the arms centrally above and bind securely into place (diagram 2).

For each sleeve, cut a 3 inch length of triple-frilled lace, fold in half, right side inside, and join the edges for 2 inches from the lower edge (two frills), leaving open above. Turn to the right side and fit over arm, seam underneath: take the divided lace at the top behind and in front of the body and then join the top corners at waist level on the opposite side of the body. Repeat with other arm, so that the top edges of the two sleeves cross over to form her bodice. Gather each sleeve level with the top edge of the centre frill, and draw up tightly round arm.

Cut an 18 inch length of triple-frilled lace for the skirt and stitch the lower edge of the flat lace along the top edge of the frilled lace. Join the two cut edges (right side inside) for centre back seam, and turn to right side. Gather the top edge of the flat lace and draw up tightly round the waist, stitching through the body to catch top edge of skirt centre front securely in position.

Gather a 6 inch length of tinsel lace across the centre, draw up tightly and stitch to back to form wings, as illustrated.

Make a small hole in the table tennis ball and paint with flesh-pink poster colour. When dry, push the top ends of the two body pipe cleaners up inside and slide head down to top of bodice. Trim neck with silver lace.

To make the hair, wind 3-ply or 4-ply wool ten times round a a 5 inch deep piece of card. Slide gently off card and tie at the centre. Stick across top of head to hang down at each side as illustrated. Then wind the wool thirty times round the card. Tie the loops at each edge with a 6 inch length of wool. Slide

The Fairy Princess. Shown here without her tree in her delicate lace dress and crown.

gently off the card and tie the centre loosely with another piece of wool Stick this tied centre over the top of the head, behind the previous piece, then bring the loops down, sticking at each side, and tie the hanging ends of wool tightly together at nape of neck: trim off surplus.

Draw eyes in black, as illustrated (diagram 3).

Join the cut ends of a 4 inch length of silver braid to form crown, then fix into position on top of head with tiny pins.

Cut two motifs from silver braid (or use silver stars) and stick together with the tip of a cocktail stick between. Cut other end to length, and stick wand to inside of one hand.

Father Christmas place setting

The advantage of this merry Santa is that although it's a straightforward flat figure for streamlined mass-production – he's free-standing: a box at the back contains sweets or a little gift for small guests to take home.

Names to indicate where each child should sit at table are written on coloured circles which can be removed once the children have found their sets. Dress Santa in felt or coloured paper – or just use paints.

Materials: Thin white, and coloured card
Red and black felt or paper (or poster paints)
Cotton wool
Gold or silver foil
Flesh-coloured poster paint
Black ink, paint or felt pen
Fabric adhesive

Method: Fold a sheet of tracing paper in half, place fold along line indicated on diagram and trace. Turn the folded paper over and trace the other half of the figure from your first outline: follow the rounded side of the hat at one side and the point at the other. Open out tracing and transfer (by rubbing over the back with a soft pencil and going over the lines with a hard point) to thin white card. Cut out. Paint the face and hands flesh colour.

Trace patterns for his hat and suit, following the broken lines across the neck and legs. Cut in red felt or paper and stick to the card figure.

Trace patterns for his belt and boot: cut in black and stick to figure in the same way. Cut a $\frac{1}{2}$ inch square of stiff paper with a hole in the centre for his buckle: cover with foil and stick to centre of belt.

Stick cotton wool round sides and lower part of face for his

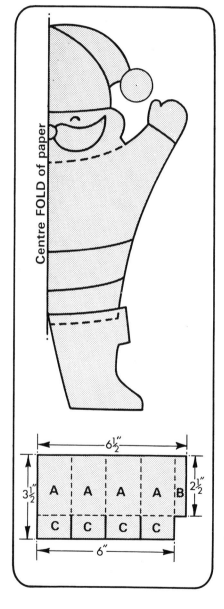

beard, as illustrated. Stick a strip across lower edge of hat and a tiny ball on the tip.

Cut the nose and moustache section in stiff white paper. Cut a circle of red felt or paper and stick to centre, then stick moustache over top edge of beard. Draw eyes in black.

To make the box, cut a piece of card $6\frac{1}{2}$ inches by $3\frac{1}{2}$ inches and mark into four $1\frac{1}{2}$ inch wide sides (A), with a $\frac{1}{2}$ inch overlap (B), as shown in the diagram. Score the broken lines, then fold sides round and stick overlap. Fold up the base sections (C) and stick. Stick box to back of figure, level with the base, leaving $\frac{1}{2}$ inch unstuck at the top.

Cut a 3 inch diameter circle of coloured card. Write the name across the top, as shown, and slip down so that it is held between the figure and top of box.

Happy Christmas tree

A seasonal decoration for a festive table: glass beads and silver balls sparkle in the candle or lamp-light as you enjoy Christmas dinner. And it's easy enough to keep the children busy in that seemingly endless period when they're wondering if Christmas will *ever* come!

Materials: Green crêpe paper
Stiff cartridge paper
Paper or polystyrene cup
Tiny coloured glass beads
Silver foil
6 inch long thin garden cane
Plasticine
Do-it-yourself adhesive

(*Left*) The Father Christmas place setting. (*Right*) the Happy Christmas tree.

Method: Cut a 9 inch diameter semi-circle of stiff paper and measure $4\frac{1}{2}$ inches as indicated in the diagram, marking the broken line to indicate extent of overlap. Curve paper round into a cone-shape and stick overlap.

Cut 1 inch wide strips of green crêpe paper *across* the grain, then gently stretch one edge by pulling with the fingertips to form a frill. Beginning at the lower edge of the cone, stick the straight edge of the crêpe strips round it, spiralling upwards so that about $\frac{1}{4}$ inch of each frilled edge extends below the strip above. Complete the tip with a frilled strip only $\frac{1}{2}$ inch wide.

Make a star from silver foil or Christmas tree decoration, fixing at the top with a silver sequin, if liked. Then thread a needle with a length of cotton and, working from the inside of the cone, stitch loops of coloured glass beads to decorate the outside, as illustrated.

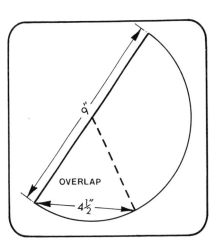

To make the silver balls, cut $1\frac{1}{2}$ inches squares of foil. Shiny side outside, turn the corners roughly to the centre, then crumple into a tight ball. Stitch between the loops of beads in the same way.

Cut away the top of the paper or polystyrene cup, leaving the base $1\frac{1}{2}$ inches deep. Roll strips of Plasticine round and press down to half-fill the base. Push a 6 inch cane into the centre so that it is firmly held, and fix a little Plasticine to the top, moulding it into a pointed tip. Lower the cone over the stick, securing it in position by pressing it down on to the Plasticine.

Stained glass snowflakes

Snowflakes–no two ever the same–in vivid colours which glow like stained glass when hung against a window or with a light behind. Either string them to hang as an ordinary mobile–or follow my version, and mount them on a sheet of clear cooking film.

If you haven't any coloured tissue papers, use coloured Cellophane or paint greaseproof paper with water colours (though this will be more opaque, so not quite as effective).

Materials: Black cartridge paper (medium-weight)
Coloured tissue papers
Clear cooking film (18 inches square)
18 inch long thin garden cane
Fine cord to hang
Do-it-yourself adhesive

Stained glass snowflakes.

Method: Cut a 4 inch diameter circle of black cartridge paper for each snowflake. Fold it in half across the centre, and then into quarters, with the outer edges and the folded edges absolutely level.

Snip away small areas along each folded side edge, as diagram, allowing at least $\frac{3}{8}$ inch of black between each cut area. Finish at the outer edge with a curve or point, and either leave the centre or cut it away as you like.

Open out the paper and then re-fold, exactly between the previous folds, sides and outer edges level, as before. Snip away shapes along the folded edges, as previously.

Open out the cut circle and press under a warm iron to flatten.

Decide on the colour scheme of your snowflake–two or three colours are best, as illustrated. Cut pieces of tissue paper large enough to overlap the black area round the section you are covering: cut two pieces of tissue together.

Spread a little adhesive over the black paper round the area

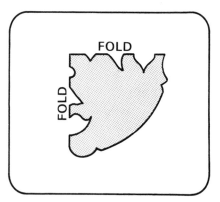

FOLD

FOLD

you are covering and smooth the tissue into place. This will be the back of the snowflake. Continue to stick tissue over the cut-out sections until it is completely covered.

Stick one edge of an 18 inch square sheet of clear cooking film round a thin garden stake. Tie a length of fine cord at each end to hang. Then stick the back of each snowflake to the film, as illustrated.

Christmas gift name tags

A pretty gift-tag makes a present so much more attractive – but they can become quite a considerable additional expense at Christmas-time, when you're labelling any number of gifts. So here's a quick way to make your own – as many as you need, for next to nothing!

Materials: Gift-wrap paper (or old greetings cards or other
suitable illustrations)
White or coloured plain thin card
Gold or silver tinsel gift-tie
Wallpaper paste

Method: Carefully cut round the edge of your chosen motifs. Then paste them to the card, either separately, or grouping two or three small cut-outs.

When dry, cut the card, roughly following the shape of the motif, but making sure the shape of the card makes an attractive and practical tag.

Punch a hole near the top. Fold a 9 inch length of tinsel gift-tie in half and loop through the hole.

Write your message on the back.

Acknowledgements

I would like to thank the following for their kind assistance in the preparation of this book:

Copydex Limited: Copydex do-it-yourself adhesive

Sellotape Products Limited: Sellobond clear all-purpose adhesive
Adhesive tapes

Harbutt's Limited: Plasticine modelling clay
Plastone self-hardening material

Binney and Smith Limited: Finart wax crayons

W. H. Smith Limited: Stationery and artists' materials

F. W. Woolworth Limited: Household and general items

Arts and Crafts:
10 Byram Street,
Huddersfield, Yorkshire
General craft materials and candle making equipment

Candle Makers Supplies:
Beaconsfield Terrace Road,
London W.14
Candle making materials and equipment

Nowadays Limited:
40 Church Street,
Leatherhead, Surrey
Who kindly loaned many of the props used in the photographs